water

LIVE AND LEAD WITH INTEGRITY

ANDRÉ KILIAN

'Water: Live and Lead with Integrity' by André Kilian

Copyright @ 2022 André Kilian. All rights reserved.
www.besoulful.co.za
andre@besoulful.co.za
Stellenbosch, South Africa

Graphic design by Elmien de Wet
www.elmiendewet.co.za

ISBN: 978-0-6397-2630-4

Printed in South Africa by Print on Demand
First Edition

*With immense gratitude to
Ilana, Cara, Theo, Jean and Luc,
as well as to Stephan, Herman, André,
Hendrik, Rudolph, Chris and Deon
who started this conversation.*

Brian and Danah - I am standing on your shoulders.

The WHY and HOW of this book

This book is for human beings searching for ways to live, lead and work with authenticity and integrity in a world of change, turbulence, deadlines and lack of time. It is a humble story of synchronicity, awakening, resistance and response. It wants to support you with simple, sustainable and practical habits towards integrity and humanity.

It is a story of awakening by chance, leaving home, meeting people, and crossing thresholds. It is a journey of shifts that happened, with wilderness experiences along the way where I was confronted with myself and my ego, realising it is really about space and humanity. And I had to respond!

I invite you to participate and respond in your own way.

You will be asked to respond to questions while reading through this book. Each chapter has space for journal reflections, with a question guiding you to respond with integrity. Through this you will create your own integrity manifesto to take forward on your journey through leadership and life.

Enjoy!

INDEX

1. A moment in time …	11
2. The water drop	19
3. Who's calling?	25
4. A mentor	33
5. It found us	49
6. Shift happens	67
7. Desert experience	77
8. It is not about me	89
9. Space happens	105
10. The way back	125
11. Just start!	141
12. Reflections	157
MY MANIFESTO	163
MINDMAP	164

Do not simply read this book.

I invite you to walk with me and to respond in your own way to this journey towards integrity. Through the humble story told in this book I want to facilitate a process aimed at helping you find your own integration.

If you are struggling to find ways to be authentic and get to the things that are really important to you, this might help. Whether you are running a business, leading a family or just living life this will invite you to ask questions about God, about yourself and about the world. You will be invited to search for your own authentic voice in order to find the 'drops of water' along the way. In the process you will capture your own integrity manifesto.

So, please don't just read the book; join the journey.

1.
A moment in time ...

> We live between the act of awakening
> and the act of surrender.
> Each morning, we awaken to the light
> and the invitation to a new day
> in the world of time;
> each night, we surrender to the dark
> to be taken to play in the world of dreams
> where time is no more.
>
> JOHN O'DONOHUE

In a world of turbulence, change and multiplicity it is sometimes challenging to keep perspective. We hear stories of trauma, corruption, climate change and pandemics, making me wonder if it is still possible to live a life of integrity (and simplicity). What does it even mean?

A moment in 2014 provided me with part of the answer and made me believe, with John O'Donohue, that there are invitations into light and integrity every day. Every single day.

Is integrity a choice, or a set of rules? Or is it about ethics? We know that life cries out for good conduct, sound choices, love, honesty, people with character, and authentic human touch. Do we still believe people are good? Management thought leader, physicist, and philosopher Danah Zohar in her book *Spiritual Intelligence: The Ultimate Intelligence* stated that "It is good to be good", making the point that good people in business are successful anyway. For me, it is a challenge to live with awareness and balance, and to stay close to what is important to me amidst the rush of everyday life. It is a challenge to try to live a life of integrity.

Yuval Noah Harari, in *21 Lessons for the 21st Century*, which is his third work after *Homo Deus* and *Sapiens*, talked about the challenges that we face in the world of the Fourth Industrial Revolution, technological disruption and data-driven change. He mentioned themes like humility, meaning, ignorance, justice, equality, and liberty. But what about lessons in integrity? Isn't that one of the greatest challenges – the challenge of integrating one's inner and outer lives? Authenticity means to live with the inner and outer parts of life aligned and connected. This raises various questions:

Why is integrity so important? How is it fostered?

Is it a choice? Does religion and faith help?

Does it depend on genes?

Who decides, and what role does pressure, survival, and threat play?

And what is the interplay between my inner life and outer life in a journey of integrity?

How do I find a way back to my ethical self?

An impossible moment

One of the things I do annually to help me with awareness, balance and alignment between my inner and outer life is to follow a 40-day email series with a spiritual thinker – Brian Draper, during Lent each year. This email series goes out to hundreds of people around the world. For 40 days, I join an intentional community. For 40 days, I keep the discipline of creating space for this daily reflective email where Brian brings me back to simple stuff like breathing, and noticing what I am grateful for, and what is important in my life. Each day, all the participants have the opportunity to reply (RSVP) with personal reflections, if they want to. Through this, an online community share thoughts and experiences, and journey together.

It was late at night on 13 March 2014 when an extraordinary awakening happened after one of these replies. Totally "by chance" and unexpected. But nothing is by chance, is it? I replied to the reflection of the day with the topic "Inside out", commenting about the challenge for me to move (shift) from mindfulness to soulfulness, and to really live integrated in the now (the inner and outer integrated). Brian normally does not reply to the RSVPs because there are too many people on the list. But the next day I received the following direct reply from him:

> *"André, have we spoken about this subject of the shift between mindfulness to soulfulness? Remind me, because if not we are syncing powerfully."*

So it happened that two people, within the same couple of days, on two continents some 12 000 kilometres apart, came to the same word, the same moment of awareness and awakening – both moved and excited. Both influenced for life. A soulful moment of synchronicity. How could this be?

Brian passionately told me how he had spent his last week discovering the idea of soulfulness and how he was focusing on the deeper shift into soulfulness from mindfulness. He said that he would be speaking on this topic at a conference in Italy because "soulfulness is so important for such a time like this in the world".

I was stunned. No, we have not talked about this ever. I was moved. If I think back to this moment, it is quite difficult to describe. It was a moment that almost could not be, an impossible moment. It was the moment where I felt a connection between my inner and outer journey – and I was astonished by the synchronicity between two people 12 000 km apart.

How did that happen, you might wonder? The same deepening thoughts and the same word appearing in two different journeys and on two continents? It must mean something, right?

This moment influenced my journey with soulfulness immensely. By chance? There is no way that I will see this as a "by chance" event. So let me tell you how this happened, and what has happened prior to that evening in 2014, because it brought about a shift in my life and my work. I do believe that a life of integrity and simple, sustainable habits is possible. And integrity is not a destination; it is a journey. It is not a 10-step plan that one can package and sell. It is a process of inner awareness and integration, which translates into behaviour and habits.

For me, it started in South Africa in the summer of 2010 when a drop of water came from nowhere. By chance? No chance! I hope that this humble story will also resonate with you where you need to find your awakening (integrity) in life and work. This is part of my response – soulfulness is about moving from deeper awareness to a deeper, unique and creative response. My writing of this book is part of this response. In each chapter I will share a simple learning called *Water drop*.

What I want to share is part of my journey moving from spiritual intelligence to soulfulness, and from ego to soul. I also want to share the conversations I had along the way, and possible applications. I have never intended for this to be another self-help model or how-to book, but rather a gentle nudge on your own journey to find your own practical steps in the art of living wisely and to find your balance in a world where meaning has become the new money. This book wants to nudge you to become aware of your moments of integrity where your inner and outer journeys dance together.

Stop for a moment ...

> *Think about the following before you read on:*
>
> *Do you want to live a soulful life with integrity where your inner and outer worlds dance together?*
>
> *Do you want to be a soulful leader wherever you are?*

Step back,
take a few deep breaths, pause
and reflect on these questions.
Do it now.

Slowly breathe in and out then read the above questions again. Pause with each question.

Breath represents the connection between the inner and outer parts, and the path of life.

We need to breathe in to stay alive. But do you just live to breathe? I hope not. I hope that you use your soulfulness to live with meaningfulness, purpose, and impact in the world. When you slowly breathe in and out it represents the connection between the inner and outer path of your life.

An invitation to participate

> *From Chapter 3 onwards, each chapter will end with a journal reflection and what I call your "response slogan" aimed at guiding you towards a journey of integrity. This will help you to not just read the book but to capture what is happening to you and what your unique response is. I do not want to be too prescriptive about this. Simply be open to what emerges for you. If you want to, these personal reflections can serve as your integrity manifesto once you have worked through the book. There is an exercise at the end.*

It all happened on an ordinary summer's day
in a township in South Africa ...

2.
The water drop

The story behind the story...

This journey was born in Nomzamo township in Lwandle near Strand in the Greater Cape Town area of South Africa.

One ordinary summer's day in February 2010, it was a Thursday, I was driving to work at Ikhwezi Clinic in this specific township. I worked as a mentor doing therapeutic group work with nurses at the clinic. Like most other days I was driving from my context, that of a white South African middle-class man who has benefitted from apartheid, into another context, that of a poor, informal settlement that was overpopulated, previously disadvantaged and still disadvantaged. I was behind schedule and late as usual, rushing to get through the traffic to meet the group.

As I drove into the clinic's parking area, my only focus was to get from my car to the front door of the clinic as quickly as possible. As I got out of the car, checking that I had my car keys, cell phone, wallet, notes and portable CD player, I locked the car. As I walked around the back of the car, I suddenly felt an ice-cold drop of water on my arm. I stopped for a moment to check where this was coming from, only to find that it came from the outside unit of an air conditioner on the precast building. For a moment I stopped at the rear end of my car to see what was around me. I saw a shack on my right-hand side with washing hanging from a hand-made washing line. I saw a mother sitting at the front door of the clinic with her sick baby on her lap. I saw kids playing in the street. For a moment, I stopped and became aware of what was going on around me. My senses sensed, I heard, I saw ... In that moment, I saw everything around me.

I then facilitated the group session at the clinic. An hour and a half later, as I came out of the clinic, I again chose to stop for a while at the back end of my car (although I was late for the next appointment), just to observe and be aware. I stopped to notice what was going on around me as I remembered the drop of water that stopped me in my tracks.

This experience took me on a journey of awareness – a journey to reconnect with my values and to live in a more aware way, more connected to God, myself and the world – not giving in to the rat race that society offers as the norm. We are so used to people saying, "Don't just stand there. Do something!" A while ago, I came across an author saying, "Don't just do something, stand there!"

That is what I did that day in the summer of 2010. I stood there and noticed. I took a moment to be aware, to see what was going on around me. This is where my journey with integrity or spiritual intelligence (SQ) started, or maybe continued. This is where I started challenging myself (again) to live more spiritually intelligent in relationships, more self-aware in work and life in general, to align my life with what I believe. I started to challenge myself to deliberately stop every now and then, and to think why something is valuable or important to me. Why did I value a relationship? How do I make something meaningful? How do I take experiences with me? In hindsight, this was a precursor to that impossible moment in 2014 when two people stumbled upon the same word.

By deliberately experiencing this story in my life, I invited the content of my faith tradition into my thinking without even thinking about it. It happened intuitively. The drop of water could not do anything on its own to move me and to transform my thinking and acting. I interpreted this according to my main narrative, and this made me more aware of my own meaning making that I apply to my world. For me, my own spirituality informed this meaning system, namely to live in the presence of God every day as an aware human being – not allowing meaningful moments to slip by but to embrace them with body and soul. To celebrate what is right with the world and not just to complain about what is wrong with the world. It is not without reason that we are called human beings instead of human doings!

It is my hope that this journey will inspire others and help them to live more aware, more whole, and more engaged in the world. With integrity maybe?

Surely, moments like these can help us to become part of the solution instead of the problem in a world full of complexity. But how?

Soulfulness was given to me in 2014 when that moment of synchronicity just happened. It started with an awakening in 2010 when a seemingly meaningless drop of water stopped me and called me. From that day it was a call to adventure, a scary adventure at times with lots of resistance and refusal, but also opportunities for intentional choices. And I want to invite you to make a choice:

> *Will you choose to become aware of the awakenings, the drops of water in your life?*
>
> *How can this help you to live with more integrity?*
>
> *How will you find the dance between your inner and outer journeys?*

This is the interplay between awakening and surrender that John O'Donohue described; this is how are we challenged by the light and the darkness. Every day, every moment, there are possibilities for light and darkness. The interplay between the two is the dance of the inner and the outer, and the search for integrity.

But this drop of water must have been a step towards something, right? It was a call to leave home! But who was calling?

3.
Who's calling?

Home is a place you grow up wanting to leave,
and grow old wanting to get back to.

The big truth for men is that often we have to leave home
in the first half of life before we can return home
at a later stage and find our soul there.

RICHARD ROHR

I was called to leave home. Home was the status quo, the comfort zone of unawareness, the mindless rushing and running. Home was what I was used to. And then the call came. First, I was called by a little drop of water on an ordinary day, and then by a book. It is amazing how you sometimes pick up something like a book by chance (never!), and it calls you towards something you have known for a while – like an awakening that is repeated again and again, nudging you in a direction. Remember that word – NUDGE!

> *Can you think of an example where you have experienced this call through something ordinary and by chance? Something that nudged you?*

A few weeks after the drop of water stopped me in my tracks, I walked past a bookshop and simply went inside to "not look for anything specific". As I stood in front of a shelf, I saw a book, *Spiritual Intelligence, a new way of being.* I have never heard of the author, but I bought it for the title and I could not put it down. Something happened between the drop of water and the buying of the book. I was called to something – not exactly sure what, but there was a nudge in another direction. Would I listen and go with it, or would I stick with my ordinary, mindless comfort zone?

I have since learned that refusal and the experience of resistance are part of the adventure. With hindsight, that day in the bookshop was part of the calling – and I had a choice to respond. If I did not respond my life would have been totally different. This nudge was a gift.

Rushing, running and life as I knew it (i.e. the comfort zone) tried to return regularly as I experienced resistance. I have learned that even with great awakenings life does not wait for you. The expectations, ego pressure, and outer and inner games are there, never mind your intention. Life does not give you a chance to stop and smell the roses, or to take a year off for a sabbatical or a retreat. The challenge was to adapt and change on the go, and to find the water drops on the way. Intuitively, I resisted this idea and opportunity because the comfort zone was easier – even though I knew the nudge was calling me. But I had to push through; I had a choice not to stay in the comfort of the known.

You will be called and you will resist

I recently worked with someone who had a lot of questions and negative emotions about mid-life. He was 42 years old and started a business that was really successful in the financial industry. Yet, he felt down and without any energy. He doubted himself for not being grateful for what he had, and this translated into physical pain. When we explored where he was in his life, he mentioned that he just knew that there is something more and that he has known this for a while. But he needed security for his family, and he liked his comfort zone. He had to give himself permission to be down about this without judging himself. And he had to name the calling away from home and the resistance and fear – this was enough of a nudge to take the next step. Today he still runs his successful firm but created space for his calling. Suddenly, he had much more energy and meaningfulness, and his business flourished even more. He was called away from home, resisted, and had to make a choice about his comfort zone.

Have you ever experienced this call, this nudge to try something else? Have you ever been called into the "more" by some ordinary, mundane experience? And you resisted this, didn't you? Because you were afraid of the change, fearful to leave home?

When a new adventure beckons, when you feel a nudge to try something new or change direction (leave home), know that you will experience resistance. You have a choice: Do I keep going, or do I give in to the pressure and stick to what is familiar? Listen to the nudging of your soul and find the drops of water along the way! Resistance is part of it, but we always have a choice. My choice was to buy the book that day. The book was the nudge that I needed.

 ## Water drop: Transformation

In any process of transition and transformation there are subtle calls to leave the comfort zone – your home. We are set in our ways, but mostly there are gentle nudges every now and then, calling you to explore your creative self and discover new landscapes. These are glimpses of light and darkness.

For me it was a drop of water and a book, and a few other reminders that I will get to. But they were there, gently calling me to leave my home and enter a life of integrity and soulfulness. I could hear the calling because I was being open and accepting, and honest about my emotions. It had everything to do with that impossible moment in 2014.

Your unique journey

At the end of each chapter there is space to write down a few reflections. It will start with a question and/or reflection on what you have read or experienced in the chapter. It is called "reflect and respond". You will then be invited to write down a simple response to this question: What is it that you woke up to? What is that one realisation or awakening that you have had? And what are you going to do about this? You therefore need to respond with:

I woke up to _____

and therefore I will _____.

In the journey of soulfulness, a unique and practical, personal response is key. So please find your own way to do this. It does not need to be profound. You do not need to be a poet to do this. There are no prescriptions. It is simply a way to document something that is happening for you. There are more journal pages at the end of each chapter for whatever you want to capture. Just be your own creative self and start now. At the end of the process (at the end of the book), you can use all these sentences to capture your soulfulness manifesto.

Take a few moments before your first "reflect and respond" opportunity...

REFLECT AND RESPOND

Have you recently read a quote, met somebody, picked up a book or simply witnessed beauty and kindness that you knew nudged you towards something? Maybe you knew that it was a timely message, but you chose to mindlessly carry on. Try to think of one instance where you felt a gentle nudge, a calling, but you resisted or postponed. Or maybe you have started something and you stopped? It can be really simple; it does not have to be big or profound.

It is those instances where you think: "I really should …"

Stay with this reflection until you find something – it is there!

Then write a few notes in the journal pages.

Next, have a first go at your response slogan.

My response slogan:

I woke up to _____

and therefore I will _____.

4.
And then I met a mentor

*The key to being a good mentor
is to help people become more
of who they already are
— not to make them more like you.*

SUZE ORMAN

Do you have a mentor?

We all need to be aware of our need for mentors. It can be a spiritual director or a coach, a parent or even a teacher. Along the way we meet people, deliberately or by chance, who impact our direction and speak into our lives. Often, you only realise this impact much later. These are the people that bring you closer to who you really are.

It was 10.23 pm on a Monday evening in December 2011, on a train between Winchester and Oxford in the United Kingdom. I was in a state of heightened awareness and feverishly writing in my journal, trying to capture the events of the past three hours. This was the reason for my trip. Is it possible that a small drop of water can change the course of one's life? Is it possible that by chance it can create a new journey? I certainly believe so, because it is the small *by chance moments* that, if we are present to them, could have a profound effect. People told me that I was crazy to take a train from Oxford to Winchester at 5pm on a Monday evening to have a beer with a stranger. Well, sometimes it is the crazy things that bring us the most joy – and creative energy!

In 2010, after reading that book by chance, *Spiritual Intelligence: A new way of being*, I wrote an email to the author Brian Draper. In his response, he invited me to visit him when I am in the UK. That is exactly what I did.

It was towards the middle of 2011 when I submitted my research proposal for a PhD. While waiting to find out whether the proposal would be accepted, I booked a week with Danah Zohar in Oxford for a course in spiritual intelligence – a term that she coined. It was a weeklong course with the Oxford Academy of Total Intelligence with Danah Zohar. While attending this course in Oxford, I wanted to take the opportunity and go to Winchester to meet the author of this profound book I had read. I did not know the distance between the two cities.

I left the course early that Monday afternoon to catch the train. When I mentioned that I was going to Winchester people thought I was crazy. It is crazy to go from Oxford to Winchester to meet a stranger for a beer, right? But a soulful conversation followed, confirming that sometimes we need to go with our crazy intuition or maybe just sense something soulful. Brian and I met on the station platform as strangers and hugged each other a few hours later as friends. And then, a few years later, soulfulness found us. That night on the train back I wrote the following in my diary:

> *It is 22.51 pm and I am on the train back from Winchester to Oxford. I just had a two-hour conversation with a stranger over a beer. It was a meaningful conversation with surprising synchronicity. I noticed genuine questions and proper listening. It was almost like an illuminating experience, but I am really curious as to what this means. Why would I take a train to meet a stranger and be so engaged? I am so glad I made this choice, and tonight I'm experiencing abundant energy and contentment! What exactly does this mean? There must be something more to this.*

As I got back to Oxford late that evening I walked back to the hotel with music in my ears, a spring in my step, and cold wind against my face. I felt alive and vibrant. This will stay with me forever. This was a journey that I needed to continue, I thought. It was a collection of choices, sometimes crazy choices, which took me from mere awareness to response. Crazy, right? Sometimes you need to live a little!

I once heard someone say that if you are not living on the edge, you are taking up too much space. The liminal space in between is a soulful space of choices.

How come a droplet of water can change the course of one's life?

Crazy, right? Wrong!

Sliding doors–a dance between chance and choice

The small drop of water stopped me in my tracks. Looking back, some of the things happening after that were not by chance. In the movie "Sliding Doors", the main character, Helen (Gwyneth Paltrow), encounters a moment where she could either miss the train or catch the train. The sliding doors moment takes her in two different directions and to two different stories. I believe that every now and then in life we have a moment, like a hinge. This drop of water was like that for me – a hinge moment, a sliding door. This I realised on the train that evening in the UK. It might well be that I am attaching too much value to this event, but I have also learned that in the process of meaning making and awareness it is my meaning to make. I should not let the ego tell me that it is crazy when I go with my soul.

> *"The great tragedy of life lies not in how much we suffer but in how much we miss. Human beings are born asleep, live asleep and die asleep. We have children asleep, raise children asleep, handle big business deals asleep, enter government office asleep and die asleep. This is what spirituality is about: waking up."* – Anthony de Mello

This was so true for me, and I believe so true for us in this time. For me, the drop of water was a moment of awakening, a moment that pulled me out of sleepwalking. And resonance happened. Believe me, I was awake on that train that winter's evening in the UK; I was not asleep.

There was resonance and connection. Without planning it, I started on a personal journey. The research process became part of that. This process had at least three initial movements:

- The external awakening – the "water drop"
- The internal response – the intentional thinking and intuitive simple response
- The external response – booking the trip and buying the train ticket.

This was the first learning for me. The entire process started with an awakening which was given to me, which happened by chance. I did not look for it, nor had I

> planned it. It just found me. It was not a cognitive thinking process or a decision. I woke up to something that was already there. I have learned that the most wonderful awakenings happen by chance, not by choice – in the being, not the doing. And those soulful moments precede the mind, the thinking.

The choice comes afterwards; it is a dance between chance and choice.

> Recollection makes me present to myself by bringing together two aspects, or activities, of my being as if they were two lenses of a telescope. One lens is the basic resemblance of my spiritual being, the inward soul, the deep will, the Spiritual Intelligence. The other lens is my outward soul, the will engaged in the activities of life.

Thomas Merton beautifully captures the dance between the inner and outer journey, and the choice after the non-thinking chance experience which is such an important part of the awakening. My train journey and the course in Oxford were the outward responses. But I first had to be open to the inner resonance, as well as the resistance from the world, and decide if I wanted to respond. Do I listen to the deep part of the self (or to God), or to the world and business as usual? We are all called to leave home, and we have a choice. Leaving home – i.e. leaving the comfort zone or the mindless rush – takes effort. It is quite easy to simply ignore the soulful nudge and keep going with business, maybe busy-ness, as usual.

Questions about God, myself and the world

I responded to the nudge. After that, a research journey started, and I met wonderful mentors along the way. I met Danah Zohar and the author of the book (Brian Draper) in person, and also the American Theologian Dallas Willard through his work. Dallas Willard unfortunately passed on in 2013 before I could meet him in person.

They have all been wonderful mentors on my journey and I am grateful for that. I have learned about spiritual intelligence and questions on God, self and the world. I have learned that an integrated life – which is a life of spiritual intelligence or soulfulness – will always engage with questions about the image we have of God, and the way that we view ourselves and the world. The following questions helped me:

> *What is the image of God that I live with?*
>
> *How do I view myself?*
>
> *What is my view of the world?*

These are questions that guide a life of integrity. I have found that these three questions are universal. They are not necessarily religious questions. I have found that people from all walks of life ask these questions, whether deliberately or not. Also, I have engaged more and more with individuals and teams in the workplace about what they are part of (their purpose), how they view themselves (their self-image and identity), and what impact they want to have in the world (their impact). Are these not the main questions of an integrated life – a life of purpose, identity and impact? That is why these questions guide three important lines of thought in this book.

Integrity is underpinned by three questions

An integrated life continuously asks why, who and where. Why is about purpose and God image, who is about identity and self-image, and where is about worldview and impact. Integrity is guided by this interplay of questions.

Image of God (WHY)

American author and Franciscan Priest, Richard Rohr says that your image of God determines you. This is about the *why* of life. Even if you do not believe in God, you have an image of God. This question determines the way you think about the world of which you are part.

Why do things happen in the world? Who is in control? This influences your experience of your purpose and your ability to make a unique difference, and how you make choices about that. This is all determined by your image of God, or lack thereof. And integrity depends on this image!

Self-image (WHO)

Who is the person in your life that you speak to the most?

Most of our conversations in life are conversations with ourselves, right? It is about the way that we give feedback to ourselves, or the way that we affirm ourselves. It is about the ego conversation (who I am supposed to be, or what people expect from me) and the inner conversation (who I am). And I speak to myself by comparing myself to others, reflecting on my story with my own family. What does my identity consist of? Who am I?

One of the theoretical grids that really helped me to think about the human system of identity was developed by the late Dallas Willard. He has a wonderful map to describe the way the human system works, which resonates with the way I think.

He uses six aspects of the human system – thought, feeling, choice, body, social context and soul. Let me quickly describe this according to Willard:

Thought (images, concepts, judgements, inferences)

Thought is that which enables us to reach far beyond the boundaries of our environment. This is our consciousness that reaches into the past, present and future through reasoning and imagination.

Feeling (sensation, emotion)

Feeling involves pleasure, pain, attraction and/or repulsion of what is being thought of. According to Willard, the connection between thought and feeling is so intimate that the mind is treated as consisting of thought and feeling. Feeling involves how we feel about relationships, positions, food and anything else.

Choice (will, decision, character)

Choice or will could be called the spirit or the heart, according to Willard. This involves freedom and creativity, and the power to do good and evil. This is the inner consent and free will applied by free action in many conditions. Actions are a result of inner choice or will in response to various situations, and this is the heart of the human system. It is, however, important to recognise that the whole of human life is not run by will or choice alone.

The body (action, interaction with the physical world)

The body is the focal point of presence in the physical world. This is where the will's primary energy source and strength come from. The body is physical as well as social, and personal relations cannot be separated from the body. Choices are imprinted into the body and its social context as a person's character, and through this the body has a life of its own. Spiritual formation is essentially a bodily process.

Social context (personal relation to others)

Being with others in the social dimension is inseparable from inner thoughts, feelings, choices and actions. The most fundamental aspect of "the other" is the experience of God, and this is located in the social dimension.

Our soul (the factor that integrates all of the above)

The soul is the dimension of the person that integrates all of the other dimensions which form one's life. This is the deepest part of the self in terms of overall operations. As Willard puts it:

> *The soul is the aspect of your being that correlates, integrates and enlivens everything going on in the various aspects of the self. It is the life-center of the human being. The soul is the deep sense of being basic or foundational, and also in the sense that it lies almost totally beyond consciousness.*

In my story, the six aspects of the human system helped in the following way: There was an external entity (the drop of water) which influenced (touched) me. This triggered thoughts as well as feelings and experiences with me. Based on this, I chose to respond in a certain way, and this energised in my body. The social context was impacted through interactions with mentors and others, and all of this was integrated by the soul – what happened was (is) soulful.

Worldview (WHERE)

The self with the image of God lives in a world. Impact in the world is about how I respond in terms of where I am. The way in which I view my own responsibility in the world determines how I will act and whether I will experience influence and impact. We all live in a specific context, and this again relates back to purpose. And the human system lives soulfully in a specific context.

So, what might (the) soul be?

Where do I draw from when I refer to soul? The reference here is not your soul that goes to heaven when you die. Here, soul refers more to the depth of your being – the space where everything comes together. Soul is the place and space of deeper unified experience and reflection, the depth of your being. We all have this, regardless of our different belief systems and faith constructs.

Soul is all about humanity

I have learned about the soul from various scholars.

Theologian, John De Gruchy wrote about faith seeking answers. His emphasis is on dynamic human uniqueness which has to do with humans becoming more human through engagement with others and the world. *Soul is the inner complexity in relation to the body and in relation to others.* This emphasises the integration of self, others and the world in relation to being human. And being human in the complexity of this world is difficult.

> I've learned this about soul. Be human!

Soul is that which makes us distinct and helps to convey the mystery, complexity, dynamics and dignity of being human, and becoming more human in a dehumanising world. There is a natural reaction to the deeply felt need to connect with our soul, or the "spiritual side" of life. This cannot be suppressed indefinitely. Fundamental aspects of life – such as art, sleep, sex, rituals, family, parenting, community, health and work – are all in part soul functions, and they fail to be meaningful as soul diminishes. Dallas Willard talked about a soulless life, which is really possible. However, it is more the diminishing soul – it is always there, just suppressed. This would explain why meaning is such a problem for people. Meaning is fundamentally a matter of transcendence. The soul is like an inner stream which refreshes, nourishes and gives strength to every other element of our lives. When that stream flows properly, we are refreshed and content in all we do, because our soul is rooted in God as the source (image) and His kingdom (world). Meaning is what we are looking for.

Dallas Willard described the soul in the following way: *The heart of the matter is when we refer to someone's soul, we are saying something about the depths of their being, something different from the self, seen in terms of desires, wishes and preferences.*

The heart of the matter is about listening to the gentle nudges of the soul, the depth of being that often happens by chance. We have a choice: Do we listen and respond, or not?

Is it possible that a random event can alter the course of one's life? Like a small drop of water? Are we open enough to see this? Or are we sleepwalking through life?

Water drop: Wake up, acknowledge the nudge, and move

I have learned to be open to meeting mentors and learning from them. I have learned it is fine to be crazy (in the eyes of the world) and take a train to Winchester to meet a stranger. I have learned to regularly and deliberately ask questions about God, purpose, identity and impact, and find ways to deliberately respond to these – even if the world thinks it is silly. And I have learned to be on the lookout for hinge moments, like sliding doors, and to make deliberate choices.

I have also learned that the external awakening happens by chance, like a drop of water. Without looking for it or planning it, it finds you in a moment of being awake. There is an internal response where you think and focus intentionally – a moment of nudge as intuitive response. There is also the external response, like buying a train ticket and getting on the train – let's call that move.

These are the initial steps (movements) of soulfulness through which you can answer these three key questions: What you are part of? Who are you? What do you need to do? It is very important that this response moment is not about giving in to the doing culture. I deliberately call it response and not action. Be careful of this! Sometimes the response is to stop doing something deliberately.

Wake up, acknowledge the nudge, and move – even if it feels silly!

Sitting on that train that night was my shift and move response. Writing this book is a continuation of that. It might be possible that a drop of water can wake you up and nudge you to shift (move). It sounds simple but it is possible.

Can it really be that simple? What really happened in 2014 in that moment of awakened synchronicity between me and someone else 12 000 km away? What happened there? And what does a late-night train between Oxford and Winchester has to do with that? Was the sliding door that I caught or missed a choice or a chance? Was I crossing thresholds without knowing it? It is my meaning to make. I did not want to believe my ego which was trying to tell me that I am crazy. This had to mean more than what I wanted to believe.

Waking up, recognising the nudge, and making a move

WAKE UP

Think about an example where you woke up to something simple. Think of a moment where you felt a life-giving energy, found something meaningful, or just felt really, really happy. Think of an *awake* moment.

Write it down.

ACKNOWLEDGE THE NUDGE

After this awakened moment, what was your thinking and internal response? Towards what did this moment *nudge* you?

Write this down.

MOVE

What would an external response look like? What is it that you need to do because of the awakening and the nudge? This can be a sliding door moment depending on your response, your *move* moment.

How can you respond to this, even if it feels silly or simple?

Write it down.

Write down your response slogan.

Put into words what has been awakened in you and how you will respond:

I woke up to _____

and therefore I will _____.

Alternatively, do a soulfulness audit by reflecting on the following:

- Your image of God, or what you are part of, or the why of your life

- Your thoughts about yourself, the conversations you have with yourself, the feedback you give to yourself, and how you view yourself

- How you experience your impact in your specific context.

For that, you need to be very specific about the place in which you live or that you occupy in life (where).

Make a few notes ...

_____

_____

_____

_____

_____

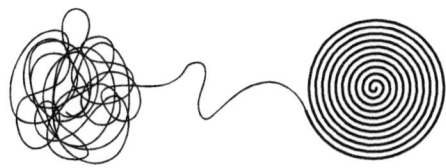

5.
It found us.

*And then, in a moment of synchronicity,
soulfulness was given to us.
It found us.*

What happened in 2014 when I had a powerful sync moment with somebody on the other side of the world? Is it possible that two people can have the same awakening so many miles apart? What does this have to do with my drop of water, and seeking to live and lead with integrity? What was that awakening, and where did it come from? The process happened sort of inside out.

Inside out

Part of leaving your home, your comfort zone and your status quo is crossing unplanned thresholds. This is an ongoing choice.

There are moments in life where awakening simply happens. Sometimes, after something had happened, you realise that it was so much more than what you expected. The evening of 13 March 2014 was like that for me – the story I told in the beginning where two people came to the same word and idea while on two continents. I replied to the "inside out" reflection, and synchronicity happened 12 000 km apart. We were syncing powerfully!

I remembered the drop of water, the sliding doors, the trip on the train from Winchester to Oxford, and the hard work of studying, meeting mentors and so on. Did all of this happen by chance because of a drop of water on a bright summer's afternoon in South Africa? There is still no way I can believe that this is meaningless. Now, three years after that "drop-of-water" soulfulness happened, it found us. That evening in March 2014, after Brian and I had realised that we came to the same word and idea while being so far apart, must be more than just coincidence. And on reflection it was a moment that, again, like the drop of water, changed the course of life and stopped us! Is this even possible?

I have been grappling with this question for a good number of years: How is it possible that two people can experience the same shift thousands of kilometres away from each other? How is this flow connected? I would love to know what the ingredients of a moment like that should be. But I won't because flow does not work like that. It just is what it is. Sometimes we simply need to accept the small miracles along the way. And lean into the moment. Because soulfulness is not always about understanding or finding reasons. Sometimes, it is just to accept the meaning, the awakening in the moment, and to experience it without understanding it. That is part of the mystery of this journey.

The threshold of "non-sense" brings a choice, again and again – how will I look at this? Will I try to explain or just lean in? Just lean in! The threshold asks for a specific way of seeing, of adjusting our eyes. This space is liminal space, a threshold between what was and what is next. Liminality is like a desert experience where it is more important to wait than to know. It is far more difficult to wait than to know.

Dallas Willard writes about how researchers decide what we know. He says that an experience is also a way of knowing: *We do not know that we know what we know!*

Therefore, just lean into the experience. Do not always try to explain it in a rational way. Experience is also knowing.

Adjust your eyes

Richard Rohr, in his book *The Naked Now: Learning to see as the mystics see,* tells a beautiful story about three ways to view the sunset. This story helped me to position my own awakening on soulfulness and to sometimes just enjoy the moment without explaining it.

> *Three men stood by the ocean, looking at the same sunset. One man saw immense physical beauty and enjoyed the event in itself. This man was the sensate type who likes 80% of the world, deals with what he can feel, touch, move and fix. This was enough reality for him, for he had little interest in larger ideas, intuitions, or the grand scheme of things. He saw with the first eye which was good. The second man saw the sunset. He enjoyed all the beauty that the first man did. Like all lovers of coherent thought, technology and science he enjoyed his power to make sense and explain what he discovered. Through imagination, intuition and reason, he saw with his second eye, which was even better. The third man saw the sunset, knowing and enjoying all that the first*

> *and second men did. But in his ability to progress from seeing to explaining to "tasting", he also remained in awe before an underlying mystery, coherence and spaciousness that connected him with everything else. He used his third eye, which is the full goal of all seeing and all knowing.*

This third-eye wisdom "happens" when by some coincidence our heart space, our mind space and our body awareness are all simultaneously open and non-resistant. It is a moment of real presence and of deep inner connection. Without explanation, just lean into the moment and embrace it.

For me the moment of synchronicity where soulfulness found us was like this – heart, mind and body unified in experience and presence. Maybe I should not anxiously try to understand *how* this happened. Maybe I should just accept the moment's wisdom for what it was.

I have learned from the journey that sometimes we simply need to lean into the experience without reasoning (like taking a crazy train ride). I often reason away all the experience, all the soulful moments, because I want to understand and control and plan. When this happens, I miss the experience, the sunset. The nudge moment should not be a moment of overthinking; it should rather be to realise what it is and to stay with it for longer, before responding. And as I have mentioned before, response is not relentless doing; it is responding to the gentle nudge.

Sometimes we can just see and taste the sunset without having to prove it. Maybe I should just see and taste the moment where soulfulness happened without the ego's need to prove it.

This was the second confirmation that the flow of soulfulness happens through being wake, noticing the nudge, and moving forward. It happened to us before we could search for it, or plan it. It found us and it woke us up. Then we talked about it and thought about it without trying to explain everything. And then we responded (moved forward), each in his own way and together. The collective response was the *Shift Happens 2016* conference, referred to in the next chapter.

In a simple moment this was given to us. We did not search for it or think about it. It just happened. It is meaningful that it happened to us, and across continents. It emphasised the importance of community and context in the work of soulfulness – it is not a theoretical, academic journey. It is about who you are, where you are, who you are with, and whether you "expect the drops of water". It is not something that you overthink or over-do. It is a gentle shift, an intentional awareness, a nudge, and a massive opportunity every time!

This was my rhythm. First a drop of water, then a call to leave home, then a book and a mentor, then crossing a boundary with a soulful sync. This threshold is such an opportunity.

The threshold is an opportunity for soulfulness

So, what then is the essence of soulfulness? Again, let us remember the three ways to view the sunset. Soulfulness is about adjusting your eyes again and again, and to move from mere knowing to wisdom.

The opportunity for soulfulness is all about the ability to integrate. One of the biggest challenges in life is to not live in compartments, but to be authentically you (or whole) in every way – to integrate purpose, identity and impact, and to live with what you are part of, who you are and where you are. Richard Rohr refers to the Latin word *integra,* which means *whole*. This is the core of the words integrate and integrity – to live as a whole.

Every threshold asks the question: How I can be true to myself, whole and live with integrity? Soulfulness is an opportunity for this. But what is soulfulness? I have deliberately referred to this in a loose way for you to form your own idea.

> *The essence of soulfulness is to "make time" for experience and inner awareness of what is really important to us (to awaken), and to translate that into a unique, creative and simple, sustainable response (nudge and move). It is the authentic dance between our inner and outer journeys.*

This is an intentional journey where you expect the water drops. This journey is guided by three questions: Who is God, who am I, and where am I? It is the rhythm of awakening, acknowledging the nudge, and making a move. It is a journey where you live with awareness of the conversation between ego and soul. I have put the words "make time" in quotation marks because it is not about making time; it is about taking the time. You cannot make time. You can only utilise the time that is there already. Soulfulness is to take the time that is there and make it count, aligned with what matters most through small, intentional responses.

Shauna Shapiro, author and professor in psychology at Santa Clara University, refers to mindfulness as three movements – attention, intention and attitude.

> *Soulfulness is about paying attention to the now, with the intention to really be present and an attitude where it you expect simple awakenings to happen.*

It is a gentle nudge of the soul. I use the word "nudge" to emphasise that soulfulness is not a 10-step process. Sometimes soulfulness happens when you change your position ever so slightly. This is why I resonate with the term "shift". Soulfulness is about gentle nudges or shifts towards something meaningful. Soulfulness is like a flow, where heart space, head space and body unify for a moment in an experience. The flow happens when we look with the third eye of wisdom. But what might this flow be about?

The flow of integrity

When Dallas Willard refers to the soul, he uses the image of an inner stream which refreshes, nourishes and gives strength to all the other elements of life. If the stream flows properly, a person is refreshed and content. Hungarian-American psychologist Mihaly Csikszentmihalyi talks about flow as "a state where one is content and has personal momentum and growing energy".

Personal momentum and growing energy cannot only be about what you DO. It has to do with BEING as well. This flow will influence doing and being, because the soul is rooted in what we are part of, our understanding of God and the view we have of ourselves. It is refreshing that this flow comes from within. In the world where the ego dominates, we buy into the idea that we are defined by flow from the outside. This means that flow is possible for anyone – within each human being there is unique potential that can be unlocked. I believe anyone can find soulful flow within their unique circumstances – and it might be simpler than you think. It might just be about being more human.

Soulfulness might be more than mind-full-ness

Brian Draper said that mindfulness is great but it can still be co-opted as a tool, and that we can end up merely servicing healthier egos. Soulfulness, on the other hand, can facilitate the real metamorphosis and birth away from ego to soul.

My water-drop experience initiated my own research on spiritual intelligence. In a moment of synchronicity, the term *soulfulness* just "happened".

I agree with Dallas Willard that knowing also happens through experience – the wisdom of knowing. When we talk about the topic of soulfulness it can easily become another theoretical description of knowing that is verified by facts.

Although this is a story about knowing through experience, I do want to share a few theoretical aspects of soul which formed part of my learning. The movement of mindfulness can easily become merely thinking about thinking without the mystery of experience – this is what soulfulness is about, the mystery of whole experience.

Integra: The soul of soulfulness

Dallas Willard referred to six aspects of the human system with the soul as integrator of this system. In addition, Zohar referred to the soul as the dialogue between inner and outer, and the communion of the rational conscious mind with the centre of the self and the centre of all being. This process and purpose of the soul point to a function of integration. *Integra* is the Latin word for whole, and it is the core of the words integration as well as integrity.

Spiritual intelligence is about living an integrated life, a life of integrity. For this we need more than only mindfulness. I propose that although mindfulness is very important, it is not enough. Mindfulness has become a popular movement. But there also is a differentiation between modern mindfulness and classical mindfulness – both valuable, though. When I propose soulfulness as a different angle I do not take away from the immense value of mindfulness; I am simply looking for a deeper, integrated resonance.

According to Daniel Louw, professor of theology, soulfulness is more than a value; it is a quality in the being function. Soulfulness is a substitute for deeper mindfulness, and it means to be more attentive to our image of God (purpose), our idea of ourselves, and our place and role in the world (context). It alerts us to wake up, acknowledge the nudge, and move. Soulfulness could mean continuous renewal, restoration and transformation.

But let us think further about the soul of soulfulness by looking at how other thought leaders have described it.

Rich descriptions of soul

In the development of soulfulness as a concept of the soul as integrator of the human system, I have learned a lot by looking at different descriptions of soul – each rich in its own way. I wanted to apply this to my own journey of soulfulness. Soulfulness is about living a life of deeper meaning without disconnecting from life, work, speed and pressure. Various authors have helped me to gain a richer understanding of soul.

Soul as meaning

American Jungian psychoanalyst James Hollis referred to the brain as the organ of thought, the heart as the organ of circulation, the stomach as the organ of digestion, and the soul as the organ of meaning. It was through the experience of soulfulness that I have found new meaning and energy.

Soul as CEO

Gary Moon, whose areas of expertise include psychology, theology and spiritual formation, referred to the soul as the chief executive officer of the human system. I find this fascinating because in an organisation the CEO is supposed to give direction, keep the business viable and close to its core, and make sure the "market" gets what it needs aiding society. A good CEO has an integrated view of the organisation. This is also the function of the soul – to guide the human system, keep it close to its core and make sure it has impact. In my own experience with the drop of water I was reminded of the things around me, and I keep that in my heart. The soul / CEO kept me close to my purpose, my identity and my impact. Likewise, the CEO has an obligation to keep the organisation focused on its meaning, purpose and identity, and to make sure there is impact.

Soul as deep self

Dallas Willard referred to the soul as the deepest dimension of the self. Zohar supported this when she referred to the soul as the channelling capacity in human beings that brings things up from the deeper and richer dimensions of imagination and spirit into our daily lives, families, organisations and institutions. The soul brings things from a deeper place into our daily lives – not our spiritual lives, our *daily* lives! Something in my deep self resonated with the drop of water stopping me and inviting me to take a closer look. Something in my deep self resonated with soulfulness and the connections that were formed through it. Soul is a dimension of the deep self.

Soul as learning

I also wanted to engage with soul theologically. Prof Daniel Louw, professor of theology at Stellenbosch University, is one of the people that significantly influenced my thinking and being. He lives soulfully with great wisdom and integration. He refers to soul as *the art of living meaningfully and a life-long journey and process of learning.* He describes soul as a collective identity and network of social systems and spiritual forces. For me, this is a journey of learning and growing, a soulful journey that forces me to shift, move and learn about myself, God, and the world.

Soul as inner frame

English philosopher Sir Roger Scruton described the soul as *the organising principle of a self-conscious creature* – like a frame that is embedded in activities and relations with individuality, personality and will. Soul is like a frame enabling you to organise yourself as a self-conscious creature. I would like to think about the ability to organise yourself intuitively before thinking. My experience with the drop of water reconnected me with this frame, and it revitalised me. Through the idea of soulfulness this inner frame strengthened and grew.

Soul as sacred space

John de Gruchy, who has lectured in theology at various universities in South Africa,, referred to the soul as central to the understanding of being human. It is *a complex embodied reality*, which gives continuity to our identity, a person in relation to others, a "sacred space" which gives us dignity and in turn provides a basis for moral responsibility, human rights, and respect. Moral responsibility happens from the soul – a sacred space within all of us. I would like to believe that this is true irrespective of your background, your story, your faith perspective, or your belief system. All of us have the possibility of sacred space inside of us. The drop of water rekindled the sacred space within me that day in 2010, and this sacred space started to resonate in different ways. Sacred indeed!

American theological ethicist William Schweiker spoke of the soul as a sacred space that gives humans the right to be respected and the right to dignity irrespective of their failures or who they are. Irrespective of who we are ... we have the right to dignity, and that is soulfully true for everyone.

These different references to soul have helped me to acknowledge the construct and use it as a meaningful way to engage with people regarding their background and what matters most to them. It is a unifying term – it does not judge or compartmentalise. And it acknowledges that we cannot define soul in one way – it is at best described in a tentative way with multiple but tentative angles. With all the above descriptions in mind, I can tentatively define soul as the following:

> *The soul is the organ of meaning, the deep-self space for learning, vitality and growth. It is the CEO, the inner frame that provides sacred space from the inside to be in the outer space with integrity in doing and being.*

This definition is a work in progress to capture something of the essence of soul, without boxing it in. The whole point of living soulfully is not to capture, name and define all the time but to work with what it is for you. That is why I keep this definition open-ended.

When the soulful sync with the drop of water happened, what happened to soul in my experience? I reconnected with meaning, with what matters most. My attention was nudged in a direction. A deeper dimension was accessed (Zohar), and sacred space was rekindled (Schweiker). It was an embodied reality for me (De Gruchy) where the CEO (Moon) was reframed intuitively and pre-thinking (Scruton). In fact, it reframed me for life. After the awakening I was moved to respond with intention, attention and attitude, in the words of psychology professor Shauna Shapiro.

Expect drops of water and let them flow

I have worked with various mentors to explore the sacred space inside each of us. We took time to awaken, shared the awakening and responded to it – we let it flow. The idea of soulfusness surfaced inside me and a mentor at the same moment on two different continents. Something synchronised and happened through us without us thinking too much and for me God was part of this. We certainly expected the drops of water. This is how it happened when I was willing to cross the threshold. I had to leave the comfort of "home", the status quo, and be willing to respond through soulfulness. I needed to be willing to learn a new language.

This is what I am trying to pass on. I am trying to remind you to be open to the drops of water in your life. Be open to the moments of synchronicity, the mentors as well as the thresholds that you need to cross. Go through life's thresholds and expect a drop of water – they are there! It is quite simple.

That is the gift that I will try to pass on.

Be realistic!

But you may ask, "Is this realistic?" Isn't the experience of soulfulness reserved for heaven or utopia? Life is complex and consists of tasks, deadlines, speed and turbulence. Surely there is no time to expect water drops and act on them? And flow? This is so unrealistic in a way because we cannot just "stop" life and take a sabbatical or a retreat. So yes, we have to be realistic. But sometimes an example of "the drop of water" can be trauma, a pandemic or a difficult life moment – it is not just beauty and water.

It is a great challenge to be realistic. But also look out for the moments within ordinary life. If I give in to the voice of security and realism, I will not experience anything out of the ordinary. I will also not see moments in the ordinary. There are water drops, people and thresholds out there that want to call you away from the ordinary. Be realistic, but also be on the lookout for those moments. Don't give in to the voice that says: "Come on, be realistic." This is what soulfulness is about.

💧 Water drop: Create space, awaken, share and respond

Intention is needed to find these moments and to create space. We need to be more intentional from this is the bare minimum.

Soulfulness gave me the language to find realistic ways to be open to life's drops of water. My soul craves meaning, and there are lots of soulful moments in every day. But I need to be open to this. I realised that there are four key concepts to make this practice realistic and to provide us with a frame for soulfulness and integrity: space, being awake, sharing, and response.

Space is really about time. Everybody is looking for time. A realistic life of soulfulness creates space (time) to be open to the drops of water that fall from the sky. The moments of meaning that happen between people, in the space between doing things.

And then you have to be *awake*. For me, this is the process I mentioned earlier in the book, and that refers to being woke and noticing the nudges – the inner awakening and the outer awakening that are happening (by thinking). This means that part of soulfulness is being in tune with your inner resonance and experience, and the way it nudges you to wake up.

In addition, it was important for me to deliberately *share* this journey. By talking to others and sharing stories we create accountability for the soulful journey. So please share your awakenings, even if it feels silly. Share them because they are significant and they need to be witnessed.

And then we try to *respond* as part of unforced flow. Small, simple responses will flow from the awakening and the sharing because you have created the space. The interplay between response and flow is important. Response can easily force you to act, or to do. Response should flow from a deeper place of soul. In responding you should be gracious with yourself to not accomplish too much. Allow yourself to make mistakes and to acknowledge the movement that is created through authenticity.

I have learned that the threshold is a place of choice and chance. Remember the dance between chance and choice? The moment of sync in 2014 is still difficult to describe and understand, but I had to lean in and just accept the experience between two people as part of my journey. This gives me great hope for a life of integrity for families, business people, couples, leaders and countries where people live with integrity. And finding a way back to the ethical self. If nothing else, the coronavirus reminded the world of this. The ethical self asks for soulful practices, being open to drops of water, and intentionality around space, awakenings, sharing and response. Living a life of response – you have a unique potential to respond with your life. This is why your responses at the end of each chapter are so important for your journey of integrity.

If you cross a threshold from the inside out, if you adjust your eyes to see with your experience, and if you move from mere thinking about thinking to soulful response it becomes more than an individual journey. You become part of something bigger, a family, a city, a country, a planet and a context – the "where" of soulfulness follows the who I am. We have to change our language collectively to find and sustain the truth of integrity.

REFLECT AND RESPOND

On creating space, awakening, sharing, and responding:

Reflect for a few moments before you move on. This is part of the practice of response to make sure that you do not just read the book but also capture your own movement.

What is soul for you?
How would you describe soul in your own life?
Provide examples and metaphors.
When last did you experience a soulful moment?
Or maybe a soulless moment? Examples?

Was it through something beautiful that you have witnessed, or a meaningful conversation with somebody? Was it a prayer, or a piece of music that stirred your soul? A sunset, a smile, or a moment of synchronicity that nudged you towards a specific response?

What was the space like? And what awakened in you?

Remind yourself that there is something sacred inside of you. Write down a few notes for yourself on the above before you move on.

Decide who you are going to share this with and when. Set a reminder if necessary.

Write down your response:

I woke up to _____

and therefore I will _____.

6.
Shift happens

*Soulfulness is about simple but deep shifts
followed by habitual responses,
supported by soulful community.*

Truth Café – no time for umbrellas!

On Thursday, 22 September 2016 I was sitting in Truth Café having breakfast with the Brian Draper, the author, after reading his book in 2010, by chance. He was here for the weeklong conference titled *Shift Happens* that we did together as part of my first effort to start a collective conversation on soulfulness in South Africa. He was the guest speaker at the conference. I decided to take him to Cape Town on the Thursday, and we ended up having breakfast at Truth Café, an award-winning, steampunk-themed coffee shop in the city centre. The name of the venue turned out to be profound – yet another example of a by chance experience which in a by chance place turned out to be part of the significance. I didn't even think about the name of the venue, just thought it would be an interesting place for him. Truth Café became a place where I discovered the "truth" for me about this week of shift. We were ordering breakfast when suddenly Brian shifted his stance and started to ask me a few coaching questions:

> *What does this week mean for you?*
>
> *What do you call this event in your life?*
>
> *Where is it taking you, and what image emerge for you as part of your journey?*

A fascinating conversation followed. When he asked me what image comes to mind when I think about the term soulfulness in my life and work, I mentioned that it feels like an umbrella. Soulfulness became an umbrella term for me regarding the work I do. I am involved in different kinds of work in different contexts. That is why I see soulfulness as a term that helps to put all my work under one umbrella. It was a unifying experience for me. But I was so wrong about the umbrella!

Suddenly, he stopped me: "No, no, that can't work." I was puzzled. I simply answered his question, mentioning the image that came up for me. An umbrella worked for me. "It can't work," he said, "because umbrellas keep you from feeling the water drops!" I was stunned. Umbrellas keep you from feeling the water drops! This is so true.

"It should be more like a wellspring" he said. Inside out, that's right. I realised that the flow of soulfulness for me is something inside of me – Shift Happens! And soulfulness became a wellspring, inside out. Ironically the title of that 40 days reflection where the moment of synchronicity happened for me and Brian was also "inside out"!

This was the truth of Truth Café!

This illuminating conversation reminded me of my first in person, with Brian that cold Monday evening in Winchester. During that conversation in Truth Café, I realised that the drop of water has turned into a fountain or a wellspring. It was part of what I couldn't help doing or participating in, and it had a unifying effect. This was my moment of integration, and integrity I suppose.

A community of truth

Part of this movement is to create a community that can intentionally stay true to what is important to them. As part of the response to my own awakening I wanted to collaborate with people in South Africa, and share stories of their experiences of soulfulness in life and work. I suppose part of my response to this drop of water was to create a community of truth that can discover soulfulness together. And together we wondered if this could become a new way of living and working. We joined for a week in September 2016 with Brian as keynote facilitator – hence our time together in Truth Café. It started in January 2014 when we had lunch in Winchester. Without thinking, I asked him if he would consider joining me for a week in South Africa. "Yes, why not?" he replied, "I've never been to Africa." And that was that.

Another story of synchronicity happened by the way, and *Shift Happens 2016* was born. Again it was me just taking a chance on a crazy idea.

Shift Happens

> *Real change is not just alterations of thought and behaviour. Real change is transformation of will and character, and it is possible but it will require an inspired CEO.*

This is my paraphrase of a quote by Gary Moon. Moon mentioned this after Dallas Willard had passed away. It is a profound statement about somebody who lived an inspired life. However, this is as true for personal transformation as it is for change management and transformation in organisations. An inspired CEO in an organisation will determine whether there is real transformation. The same applies to the role of the soul in personal transition and growth – soul is the CEO of the human system, the place for real transformation.

My personal transition became communal in 2016. I was so encouraged by the stories of leaders, organisations and individuals during that week in September. But the truth in Truth Café moved me, gave me the language with which to convey my message, and made me realise what this was. I have learned that shift happens!

American Jungian psychoanalyst James Hollis, in his book *Finding Meaning in the Second Half of Life*, said the following about finding our direction in life:

> *The task then is relinquishing the dependence on the fractal scripts for the larger project, which propels us into the direction of wholeness. When we can make this shift – and it takes the whole of the second half of life to swing our vessel around, so powerful are the old currents – then we feel embraced and supported by a large energy source again.*

This shift that happened for me resonates with Hollis's quote that shift takes the whole of the second half life. This was a moment for me, realising that shift is not an event. Instead, it is a process.

 The water drop: Shift happens

Shift happens. The year 2016 has taught me the following:

- Coaching questions can unlock your own truth when you are least expecting it.

- Soulful organisations and soulful leadership are possible.

- The community has power. Shift happens when people come together to experience things together.

- We need allies along the way.

- You need to go public with your response and you need to do this with humility – tell your story and follow your hunch. Be true to yourself.

Find a group of people – a community of truth if you like – to think and be together.

Soulfulness is an inner journey. It cannot be an umbrella. For me, it has become a wellspring, an inner space where I need to be honest with myself and be willing to listen to the wisdom of others. That was the fourth moment of significance on my journey.

First, the drop of water.

Then the book, by chance.

Then the moment of sync over 12 000 km.

And then the truth in Truth Café.

But is this possible? Although all of this happened, I was still confused whether a drop of water can really awaken real integrity. Surely, it cannot be this simple? But after every awakening there is a desert experience around the corner, making it difficult to go further and fall upward, and integrate the learning towards lasting transformation.

You see, personal and/or organisational shift does not happen outside in; it happens inside out. After an awakening, there is an inner shift that is followed by outer transformation. And we find it really difficult to have lasting change because we are waiting for external drops of water. Those do happen, but then internal flow needs to happen as well. I now realised that the shift happened inside, and that nothing would stop the inner momentum and flow. Or would it? I was so wrong.

There was a desert experience around the corner …

REFLECT AND RESPOND

Take a moment and deliberately find a space to sit down. If not now do it later today. Simply sit there and try to relax your body. Take a few deep, slow breaths. It sometimes helps to slowly breathe in, hold your breath for a few seconds, and slowly exhale.

While you continue to do this, reflect on the following:

Why are you reading this book now? What does it mean to you? Think about an image or metaphor that comes up that represents this journey (of integrity) for you. With whom can you share something of this to keep you accountable on this journey?

Make notes in your journal or the pages below or draw something.

Write down your response:

I woke up to _____

and therefore I will _____.

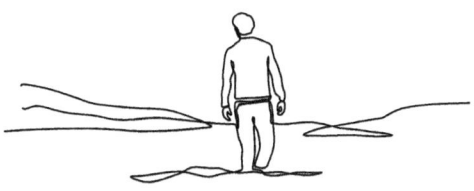

7.
Desert experience

Ready, steady, stuck

Ready, steady, stop – the desert is a liminal place!

After Shift Happens 2016, I was full of energy, ready to start a business. I wanted to build a website, design workshops and get this business going. I was so energised by the groups that came together that *I couldn't wait*. Yes, there is the dreaded sentence – could not wait.

The disease of impatience

James Hollis, in his book *What matters most: Living a more considered life,* said the following about our inability to be patient:

> *We have an entire culture of addictive treatment plans, of sensate distraction, and of jejune impatience that is driven by the preference of security through unconsciousness as an antidote to growth.*

The inability to wait – isn't this one of the diseases of our culture? The culture of instant gratification, to get everything now, is growing by the day. I just need to look at my children to realise how everything is available at the touch of a screen, and how they grow up in an environment of "can't wait".

Simon Sinek, British-American author and motivational speaker, talks about instant gratification and how, with technology, we have created a culture that cannot wait. If you do not know something, simply google it. If you want to watch something without commercials, just stream it. Everything is available with a click on a screen. But is everything instantly available? The important things in life – like being content, being satisfied with your job, love and integrity – take time. For most of these we need the ability to wait. And I couldn't wait – I wanted to move forward instantly. The wellspring was driving me to instant achievement.

I know in new business development the line between being energised by impatience and the inability to wait and discern is indeed very, very fine. A wellspring does not wait. It is so important to have an attitude of go, go, go, to be driven by energy and impatience. But there is always a risk in not waiting, discerning, thinking and let it hang for a bit. And that is what happened to me. I could not wait. I was ready to register the trademark, build the website, and design the workshops. I was too hasty. Luckily, a desert experience was waiting for me. A desert experience will always put you into liminal space that is filled with possibilities, opportunities, and wisdom. It really was a desert opportunity.

Go liminal

Liminal space comes from the Latin word *limen* which means *threshold*. This is the threshold between what was and what is next. Normally, this is a place of transition, waiting and not knowing. Yes, not knowing.

Paul Tournier, the Swiss physician who had a special interest in pastoral counselling, referred to liminality as being *en route*, having left your home and not yet having arrived at your destination. This sounded really familiar to me. This was where I was at, still *en route*. I did not know how to proceed after leaving home. But liminal space is often the state where transformation or shift happens, and where wisdom is acquired. That is, if I can learn to wait and let something happen to me. Richard Rohr writes the following about wisdom and liminal space:

> *Liminal space is where we are betwixt and between the familiar and the completely unknown. There alone is our world left behind, while we are not yet sure of the new existence. That's a good space where genuine newness can begin. This is the sacred space where the old world is able to fall apart, and the bigger world is revealed. If we don't encounter liminal space in our lives, we start idealizing normalcy. The threshold is God's waiting room. Here we are taught openness and patience as we come to expect an appointment with the divine Doctor.*

If our liminal spaces are approached intentionally and within community it will take us away from fight, flight or freeze. But I just froze. And I almost missed my appointment with the divine Doctor.

I thought I had my brand, launch-pad and a following. What could go wrong? There was the risk that it was becoming about me! My trademark "Shift Happens" obviously was sorted. What could go wrong? But one day I received a message saying that the trademark was already taken. I was not prepared to phone and talk to the guy to find out whether it was still utilised – I just froze. I went through the classic symptoms of denial, anger, and disillusionment. How could this be? This trademark or logo should be mine! Now! I sounded like a two-year-old not getting his way immediately.

The wilderness of possibility

I was forced to hang out in the wilderness, the place of wisdom – uncomfortable, vulnerable, and passive. It was liminal. And for some reason while I was hanging in the wilderness I went into a state of discernment. It became okay just to hang for a bit. It was sacred. I was forced to really think about *Shift Happens 2016*, what happened, why it happened and what it means for me. I realised that it might not be about me, and that this might just be a threshold. I had to remember the truth in Truth Café.

Eugene Peterson, an American scholar, theologian and author, used the beautiful metaphor of a trapeze artist in mid-air transit after leaving the hands of a fellow trapeze artist, expecting to be caught by another. This is a highly creative space, filled with anxiety, panic, and also expectation and energy. Certainly not boring! Peterson called it *a moment of extraordinary aliveness*. And the wilderness, the desert, certainly creates the possibility for new and surprising encounters with meaningfulness and the divine Doctor. This was indeed my liminal desert experience which I haven't asked for. It was an experience of wisdom and doubt, certainty and insecurity, faith and unfaith.

Wisdom

And the wilderness fosters integrity.

Richard Rohr succinctly wrote the following in *Falling Upward*:

> *What looks like falling can largely be experienced as falling upward and onward, into a broader and deeper world, where the soul has found its fullness, is finally connected to the whole, and lives inside the Big Picture.*

Experiences of wilderness and doubt often foster wisdom and connect you back into the bigger picture. A life of integrity is a life of integration, and the wilderness often helps you to see the bigger picture. My falling into my own anger and my impatience forced me to wait and receive the bigger picture from the wilderness. This is why Richard Rohr, in the above quote, described the experience of falling as a process of growth, i.e. falling upward. This anger, frustration and impatience in the wilderness brought wisdom and growth in the right direction. A kind of "falling" upward. It brings doubt, though. Because you sometimes fall into growth.

A friend of mine who started singing lessons at age 60 shared the story of how one day he couldn't get to a high note. His teacher then told him: "James, you do not take a high note, you fall into it." Falling upward indeed. And this falling upward process often creates doubt. The wilderness is often a place of doubt, isn't it?

Doubt is pregnant

James Hollis explained why doubt is good:

> *Doubt is a profound and effective spiritual motivation. Without doubt, no truism is transcended, no new knowledge found, no expansion of the imagination is possible. Doubt is unsettling to the ego and those who are drawn to ideologies that promise the dispelling of doubt by preferring certainties never grow.*

Doubt is part of this journey through the desert of impatience and ego. It left me with a lot of questions. Will I survive if I stay true to this? Are we even allowed to do something meaningful in our lives and make a living, make money?

Or is a life of integrity too risky?

Despite all the questions (and falling), it was a time of great learning. Through the doubt, the falling upward process was a great teacher. I have learned to stay with the question, to stay in the doubt, and to not force an answer. Sometimes the knowledge is in the doubt and the questions, not in the answers. What a great teacher doubt and wilderness sometimes are.

Out of the wilderness

Sometimes we are pressured into ready, steady, go. Then, for various reasons, things do not work out quickly enough and it feels like ready, steady, stuck.

The world tells us to be ready in order to move quickly. We must not waste time. Instead, we must drive success as quickly as possible. But wisdom is sometimes slow. Time wasted is often time well spent in the long run. The quick answer is not always the best answer. The ego wants quick, successful solutions. But these solutions are not always soulful ones.

It was in the wilderness where I have found true success in the long run, where I was honest about myself and my emotions, and where soulfulness really happened for me. I am quite sure that without this experience of stuckness and doubt, the right path would not have happened. Yes, it might have been quicker and easier but not the wiser.

Soulfulness is about being honest in the stuckness and doubt, and patiently waiting for the wisdom to come. Soulfulness is about leaning into the time in the wilderness, because out of the wilderness comes wisdom.

Canadian author and leadership expert Robin Sharma beautifully shared how time in the wilderness brings balance, energy and wisdom. He talks about *the value of alternating time* between success, drive and recovery. There is an important interplay (with hindsight, of course) between the speed, the drive to be successful and the chase, and time to recover. The wilderness often brings time for recovery.

You do not choose the wilderness; it just happens. If you embrace it, it can be a time of "falling upward", growth, and discernment. We have experienced this in 2020 and 2021 with the global Covid-19 pandemic where a lot of recovery happened during a time of wilderness. Unfortunately, this often includes pain and heartache because it is still a process of falling. I certainly wanted to make the most of the wilderness experience. In this story it was, in hindsight, the most valuable time for perspective and growth, patience and wisdom.

Water drop: The wilderness is a great teacher

The wilderness comes with many questions, doubt and struggling. Yet, it is also a great teacher – a time of great learning and falling upward.

I have learned that it should not be about me. Wisdom kicked in when I realised that I should just stand back, also from my own needs, and let things happen. Liminal space is uncomfortable. It makes you question who you are, where God is, and what your purpose is. Looking back on the journey of soulfulness and integrity, although nothing really happened, things aligned in the right way for the right reasons. The desert experience and the patience it required brought wisdom and light bulbs. I have learned that the wilderness is a place of wisdom, and that wisdom takes time.

I have also learned that I need to be aware of my ego conversations and challenge these narratives. I have learned that doubt is part of the journey, and that growth often happens in the suffering. But maybe the greatest learning was the value of patience, going slow, doing nothing, staying with the uncomfortable. Simply wait, because wisdom comes to those who wait.

However, I was about to discover the real value (or real inner shift) of this wilderness experience for the longer journey. The death of the ego was around the corner as the wilderness brought great discoveries. Soon, the ego would be challenged...

REFLECT AND RESPOND

Do the following breathing exercise:

Take a few deep breaths and try to relax your whole body.

Where is it in life that you experience limbo, liminality or wilderness?

How can you deliberately lean into that experience
and stay there for longer?

What is your ready, steady, stuck?

Make a few notes in your journal, or the journal pages in this book.

Write down your response:

I woke up to _____

and therefore I will _____.

8.
It is not about me

*The sense of rightness
comes about through the alignment
of the ego with the will of the soul.*

JAMES HOLLIS

ME, ME, ME ... maybe not

I remember a morning session at Stellenbosch Business School in 2017. A group of about 30 people gathered for their annual strategic planning process and sensed that they needed to start with something soulful before they strategised. This was just a few months after my desert experience, and I was grateful that the waiting had paid off. I followed the emails between directors and realised that they were quite uneasy. They did not know what to expect as the idea of soulfulness was not part of their theoretical and academic world. Not knowing was unnerving for them.

Wentzel van Huyssteen, professor in Theology and Science at Princeton University, said that all knowing derives from experience. Earlier, I referred to Dallas Willard's words on experience and knowledge. For a business school to sense that strategic planning needs to start with experience and being, was a big jump! It was so encouraging to me that they sensed this – to quietly go inside before strategising in the outside life.

It is important how we manage this inner and outer journey. The outer strategy depends on the inner, intuitive strategy, and soulfulness wants to align these two. In life we are forced to strategise and move. Often, we move away from our inner resources without really nourishing them. In the culture of go, go, go we are often challenged to perform on the outer journey – the risk of this is not nurturing the inner journey. Soulfulness and practices of soulfulness want to find ways to nourish the inner life, not just in personal life but even in the strategic processes of business. Work and business become much more sustainable once there is an inner flow of purpose and meaningfulness. It is like an inner stream (wellspring) that needs to have a source with good habits. Stellenbosch Business School sensed this.

At this workshop, I talked to the participants about the ego-soul conversation that happens in leadership, and the inner conversation between who you are and who you should be. I asked them to share examples of the way that they engage in meetings and teaching, work together, and "overhear" the voices inside (so to speak). I asked them to share what pressure is created in their experience of what they should be. Their responses included the following:

> "I am supposed to be in control."

> "A leader always knows everything."

> "What will they think of me?"

When I asked for feedback, one of the most senior people in the room (an obvious expert in leadership and people development) commented with tears in his eyes:

> "Today, this exercise humanised my colleagues again."

Wow, colleagues being humanised. This comment reminded me how, in life and leadership, there is so much pressure on who I need to be, and what others expect of me. It so often takes away the humanity of it all. And it often puts pressure on who I authentically am. This is also true for me – in my desert experience I was confronted with who I am supposed to be and what I should do with this business. Soulfulness is about being human again. Are we human doings or human beings? Thinking back to this business school session, I realised again how I experienced the pressure to BE someone and to deliver, to help and to create. I have learned to become aware of the ego voice inside that wants to remind me who I am supposed to be, instead of claiming my God-given uniqueness.

Another example: In August 2017 I conducted a first workshop on soulfulness with an organisation of about 20 people in the field of machine learning. I was quite nervous because we had a room full of millennials, most of them with PhDs, and I was trying to sell experiences and silence to professionals in software development and engineering. I was especially nervous about my ability to use a computer (particularly the use of slides) in their midst. During the check-in exercise I asked each person to tell me one thing about themselves that is interesting. One of the participants told me that when he walks into a room, he first checks what is wrong because he is a critical observer. Without thinking, and me being an extrovert, I immediately asked him if he had any critical feedback about the workshop so far. I asked this as a joke. Leaning forward, he answered: "Yes, I do, dude. Never use Chiller font on your first slide."

Apparently one of the main rules in slideshow design is that the font called Chiller is a definite no no on a first slide. My first slide, displaying the workshop title, was total CHILLER. A chilling shiver went down my spine and through my ego.

My ego was telling me: "Idiot, you are 40 years old and you don't even know that. This guy is 24. What will they think of you?"

This was the start of the workshop. Today, a few years later, I am on a wonderful journey with this group. They grew to 40 employees, and they are one of the examples of a soulful organisation. They quickly reminded me that I can be authentic and that I need to manage my ego talk and stay humble about what I know – or what I think I know. And to be okay with what I do not know. This inner conversation of who I am and who I am supposed to be is quite universal, and it is definitely not wrong.

Ego is not wrong!

Robin Sharma said the following: "A bad day for the ego is a good day for the soul." James Hollis, in his book *Finding Meaning in the Second Half of Life*, said this about the soul:

> *The soul is simply the word for our intuitive sense of a presence that is other than the ego, larger than the ego and sometimes in conflict with the ego. The soul is the archetype of meaning and the agent of organic wholeness.*

Me, me, me. Have we lost ubuntu?

After *Shift Happens 2016*, there was a lot of pressure to keep going, to create something and to deliver. Initially, I felt a lot of responsibility to create a brand and to start a movement in South Africa. Thankfully, the movement started but in a different way than I had expected. All of that was because of the desert experience. I experienced my ego telling me what others will think and expect.

Joseph Campbell developed the Hero's Journey in his book *The Hero's Journey: Joseph Campbell on His Life and Work.* In the hero's journey, after the desert experience, there is a central ordeal, or death-of-the-ego experience, and this was it for me. I had to realise the inner conversation, and as the trademark of Shift Happens slipped away, I had to realise that it was not about me. I am part of something else. I remembered Brian's words when he arrived in South Africa in 2016:

> *"The crucial thing is that we flow from the true self in God's grace and remember that something bigger is unfolding, in which we are being invited to participate."*

It is difficult to simply trust that I am participating in something bigger. I had to experience and be honest about this inner conversation, and the interplay between ego and soul.

The inner conversation: A word on ego

Whether you are teeing off on the golf course, making a statement in a management meeting, disciplining your children, socialising with friends, or delivering a public speech, most of us experience an inner conversation between who we are and who we are supposed to be. This inner voice reminds us of the pressure to perform, to look good, to add value, to play the game. What I choose, deliberately or intuitively, to show to the world and what I assume the world will think of that create this inner conversation. Brian Draper, James Hollis, Richard Rohr and Danah Zohar helped me to recognise and find the language for this inner conversation. And a part of my own discovery was how to stay true to myself in a world that has so many demands.

I was reminded of this by the drop of water, the book, the truth of Truth Café as well as the community of truth emerging from *Shift Happens 2016.*

This inner conversation can have different names. Maybe a true self versus a false self. James Hollis referred to the true self and the social self – the social self being the self that develops and strategises in different contexts. I quite like the idea of the social self instead of the false self. The false self can easily sound as if it is opposing the true self, as if it is something to get rid of. In conversations about spirituality the false self is often associated with sin, which you need to get rid of. In the journey of soulfulness this is not helpful. The ego is the false sense of self, emphasising that it is an interpersonal sense of who we are supposed to be. This is a sense of the other's expectations and how we project that from a place of ego.

So, what is true?

True? True self?

In each person there is a unique trueness with potential and individuality. Richard Rohr, in his book *Immortal diamond: The search for our true self*, says this is like an immortal diamond inside of each human being.

> *Life is not about creating a special name for ourselves, but uncovering the name that we have always had.*

Soulfulness and integrity are the uncovering process of life – a journey of uncovery to find and show what is "true" inside of us. This is a humbling process. Positive psychology expert Shawn Achor referred to Self 2 as the whole human being with all its potential and capacities, including the hardwired capacity to learn. Self 2 is characterised by relaxed concentration, enjoyment and trust. It wants to operate in the flow of authenticity. And the flow of authenticity is a lifelong journey, isn't it?

And what might be false?

False? False self?

The false self (or social self) might also be called the small self, or who you think you are. It is the way that you define yourself outside of love, relationships, or divine union. The ego is the part of the voice that tells you who you need to be. Rohr says the ego has three themes in this inner conversation: competition, comparison, and control. It asks you whether you are competing well enough and whether you are winning. It wants to compare you with others, and to create your identity in terms of how you compare to others. It wants to tell you that you need to be in control, with no sense of uncertainty.

Shawn Achor calls this Self 1 – the internalised voice of our parents, teachers and those in positions of authority. It seeks to control Self 2 and does not trust it. This false or social self is often characterised by tension, fear, doubt and trying too hard.

Most of us can identify with this inner conversation that sometimes creates tension and conflict. I have tested this in leadership and organisational teams, in life coaching and in therapy, and it is evident that although we are not very aware of this it influences the way we portray ourselves. This conversation is projected in every relationship, and it determines the way in which we live (or not).

But let's get practical ...

Inner conversations and overhearing.

As part of a soulful leadership workshop, I asked the teams how they experience this inner conversation and what it says to them. I asked them how they overhear themselves when the ego and soul are in conversation. Their responses included the following:

> "I have to be professional."
>
> "I have to make a contribution."
>
> "Will they like me?"
>
> "I have to have an answer."
>
> "I have to say something."
>
> "Do they think my contribution is significant?"
>
> "I need to be the expert."

I can go on and on. In all these conversations I have experienced authenticity as well as the pressure of ego talk. By sharing their responses, the participants made themselves vulnerable to each other.

Google the video "Soul Runner" by Brian Draper. It emphasises this inner conversation in a moving and honest way.

A soulful encounter between Ego and Soul

This conversation is part of who we are. It is not two selves – it is two experiences of the self, one true and one social. And the soulful encounter is to be aware who is speaking to whom. It is not a choice between true and false. It is not an effort to get rid of the ego. It is about keeping the two voices connected to the source. All is connected to the immortal diamond inside, the God-given uniqueness and potential of each human being. It is a soulful encounter within – and part of the answer in this turbulent world is to foster this soulful conversation and to recognise it. And to hold it with grace and patience.

This soulful encounter is part of the solution, and it can bring about a sense of purposefulness (purpose, identity, impact). James Hollis described this purposefulness as a sense of rightness that comes about *through the alignment of the ego with the will of the soul.* Isn't that beautiful – the soulful encounter between ego and soul can bring alignment and purpose. This alignment and awareness of a healthy conversation between ego and soul translates into integrity. It is an integrated and aligned (inner) conversation that translates into an integrated and authentic way of living, in being and in doing – being true to yourself, your unique God-given self, if you like.

Integrity comes from this soulful encounter, which might be represented by the following image.

Earlier in this chapter we referred to James Hollis's explanation that our sense of rightness happens through the alignment of the ego with the will of the soul. The picture above represents the soulful conversation between the inner and outer, soul and ego, or the authentic, true self and the social self. We are standing on a bridge between the two, holding onto both parts of ourselves (the whole self) instead of choosing only one part of our selves.

Frédéric Laloux is the author of the book *Reinventing organizations: A guide to creating organizations inspired by the next stage of human consciousness.* This book is aimed at helping us understand the development of organisational consciousness. It is fascinating how he refers to ego experiences in the workplace:

> *By looking at our ego from a distance, we can suddenly see how its fears, ambitions and desires often run our life. We can learn to minimise our need to control, to look good, and to fit in. We are no longer fused with our ego, and we don't let its fears reflexively control our lives. In the process, we make room to listen to the wisdom of other, deeper parts of ourselves.*

Making room to listen to the other deeper parts of our lives. How do we do that? How do we create space? What can we do to be more aware of this deeper, intuitive, inner conversation? It should be by creating habits and disciplines, or rhythms of grace. And the first challenge is to just be aware of this deeper inner conversation, not to fight anything. When we are not aware, competition, comparison and control are spoken into our lives.

A world of competition and comparison

When I talked to the group at the business school about this inner conversation and about the ego that wants to compete, compare and control, the director of the business school put up his hand, asking: "So, does this mean we should not compete in the business market as this is naïve?"

And this has been the question ever since with almost every organisational group. As mentioned by the professor, it is naïve to try and get rid of the ego, and it is not realistic to get rid of the competition. The question for me is whether this competition defines you or not. There is a way to navigate this, and that is through a soulful inner conversation (encounter) – which means you still compete and compare, and try to be in control, but for different reasons. As mentioned, this can be a *soulful encounter* between Self 1 and Self 2.

> *A soulful encounter between ego and soul, from moment to moment towards purpose and impact – that is a life of integrity.*

Maybe the challenge is not to stop competing and comparing, but to operate from the awareness of this inner conversation between the ego and the soul, to appreciate the authentic and unique self, and to move from:

Compare to collaborate – working together

Compete to connect – forming relationships

Control to contentment – letting go.

This means that we still compete, but with the emphasis on connection and purpose. We still compare, but in a collaborative way. And although we need to be in control, we do it from a place of contentment, without anxiety, and without control defining us. What would organisations look like that compete, compare and control from a place of purpose and authenticity? This I do wonder. While competition, comparison and control are pivotal for organisations and individuals this should not define you.

Water drop: A soulful encounter is possible!

I have learned that this inner conversation is alive and well for most of us, and that this conversation creates a lot of pressure in our social sphere. It takes people away from themselves, from their true selves. I have learned that this soulful encounter is not something I should fight. Instead, I should learn from it. I have realised that although one of my main gifts in the helping profession is to help people, this is also the biggest risk in terms of my ego talk. I cannot always help, and that is okay.

I have also learned that helping sometimes means transferring responsibility to the other person. Helping sometimes means simply creating space for awareness and reflection, allowing people to make their own choices (or not). Often, this helping process is simply to uncover the conversation between ego and soul.

I have learned that mindfulness can also be used as a self-help tool that serves the ego – we easily compete to see who is the most mindful, again a capacity of doing. Brian mentioned the following to me a conversation: "Mindfulness is great but it can still be co-opted as a tool. When this happens, we merely end up servicing healthier egos. Soulfulness, on the other hand, begins to facilitate the real metamorphosis, the birth away from ego to soul."

Soulfulness wants to "do" something else – it wants to help you encounter both the ego and soul. The dance between the inner and outer, according to Thomas Merton.

Soulful encounters between the ego and the soul can bring about healing. It helps us to be honest about this pressure of expectation, and this can aid us in leadership and living. To live authentically does not mean to live without ego experiences. This is impossible, I would suggest. It is about being aware of who is speaking to whom inside of you, and for what reasons. This calls for a healthy conversation. It wants you to believe that you are not defined by competition, comparison, or control. It wants you to love your true self, the unique immortal diamond inside of you. This means to be more okay with vulnerability, even in the workplace.

When last have you affirmed the you of you? The God-given self that is unique to you – without your sense of who you are supposed to be or what others expect of you? This is what I have learned: Make space for the soulful encounter inside with grace, humility and patience. Soulfulness is about creating this space!

And even with all this wisdom I still wonder: Is it possible that a small drop of water can do all of this? Is it realistic? What does this soulful encounter mean for my day-to-day life, and how do I apply all of this? Is it a choice, and how does that make me live in a more integrated way? I realised with the death of the ego comes wisdom …

Maybe it is not about me. Brian's words echo in my head: "Remember that we are participating in something bigger." But what might this be?

It is all well to experience the inner life. But how do we translate this into outer life? Realistically? Rush, run, integrity? This was my realisation and inner shift!

REFLECT AND RESPOND

I invite you to try this:

Think about the conversation between ego and soul (refer to the picture on page 98) that you experience inside of you every day. What is it that you overhear? In which areas of your life are you experiencing pressure in terms of who you are and who you are supposed to be? Where do you experience the "me, me, me" pressure? Think intimate relationships, management team, parenting, and social interactions?

Try and affirm something unique about the *you* of you, the God-given immortal diamond inside of you. Write this down in your journal or the journal pages of this book.

Write down your response:

I woke up to _____

and therefore I will _____.

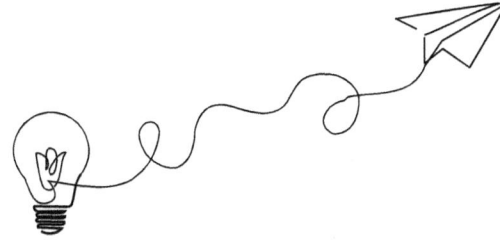

9.
Space happens

The soul is spacious, plentiful,
and its amplitude is impossible to exaggerate ...
the sun here radiates to every part ...
and nothing can diminish its beauty.

ST TERESA OF AVILA, THE INTERIOR CASTLE

I'll be with you in a minute. I just quickly want to …
Does that sound familiar?

We are filling our space with tasks. Mindfulness expert Jon Kabat-Zinn wrote about our "frequent impulse to always squeeze in another this or another that into a moment". Just another phone call or just another stop on the way. "It has me unavailable to others at those times, missing the play of light on the table, the smells in the room and the energies of the moment" – in Kabat-Zinn's words.

This is so true. Our busy-ness often leaves us unavailable to others. We are always scheduling, helping, saving. We find it difficult to just be. There is no space to just be.

Are you uncomfortable with too much space? Or are you really longing for more space? Are you longing to just be available to the people around you, and to the soulful opportunities waiting in the sunset, the smell in a room, or in silence?

The longing to help

This is the story of how my longing to help people was often fuelled by this impulse to *do* another thing. This has now shifted, allowing me to embrace space again – space to observe, sense, listen, smell and be available, without the urge to always help. But during the first part of my life, I jumped to always help and please in an urgent way. It was a longing to be of help, and to be available and attend to whatever the other person needed.

My worst nightmare is when if I know one of my children is suffering, and they do not give me the opportunity to help them. One day, we realised that our 12-year-old daughter was battling with something. We really tried to engage with her, motivating her to share with us what is bothering her. One evening when my wife and I again entered her room to try and reach out to her, she firmly told us that she believes one should sort out one's own problems: "I am choosing not to tell you everything and will deal with stuff on my own. So, deal with that!"

Those words will haunt me for a good few years. At the same time, it helped me to think about and deal with my urge to always help. This was part of my soulful encounter between the ego and the soul, and it rocked me to my roots. That is why I do what I do – I help people. I take it very personal when somebody, especially a child, denies me the opportunity to help. My life always has been about helping people. This is a great gift, but it also comes with a big shadow. Often, if you think your only mission in life is to help, and you are always fixing others, there is a real risk that you are not looking after yourself and that you are taking on too much responsibility.

Is your identity based on your eagerness to always be available to help? Is this feeding your ego? These are the questions I had to ask myself. The shadow side of this is taking on too much responsibility. Although I might have helped somebody else, it is still really about me, me, me.

The soulful journey helped me to realise that I cannot and do not always have to help people. (Sorry, mom!) Sometimes it is okay and even profound just to create space for others. It is okay to trust that what will happen will happen, and that I am not responsible for all the help. Creating space to sense, smell and be silent can go a long way in helping people to solve their own problems. It is like enjoying the sunset that is already there without trying to clarify or change it.

We are only participating in something bigger, aren't we?

Finding space

Space is a wonderful thing. But it is scarce. We crave for space on different levels – space to recharge, to dream and to be creative. The world is turning into a toxic machine that is running faster and faster, taking up more and more of our space. Our space and creativity are stifled by structure, planning, control, competition, and the workings of the ego. Predict and control.

Where do you still have space to dream and imagine things?

Just to have wild bog dreams and time to breathe?

> *Think for a moment ...*
> *When last did you really experience space?*
>
> *Think of a simple example where you've really experienced space? Be specific.*

Isn't it true that space often happens in the outdoors and nature? A few years ago, I took a group of leaders to a labyrinth at Rustenburg farm just outside Stellenbosch, South Africa. At one of the pause points I asked them to deliberately look at the leaves of an old oak tree and focus on the space between the leaves, not the leaves themselves. Afterwards, one of the participants commented: "Wow, I cannot believe what happens if you deliberately create space!"

Isn't it true that music is made up of notes as well as space between the notes?

In life it is often the space in between that creates the meaning. Sometimes it is the space that is created through death and trauma that gives people new perspective. Space is often not planned, but I've learned that soulfulness is about intentionally creating space and then being open to what happens in this space. This space holds gifts. We can learn and grow from these spaces.

Richard Rohr described the journey into the true self in his book *Falling upward: A spirituality for the two halves of life* in a beautiful way:

> *You do not climb up to your true self, you fall into it, so don't avoid all falling.*

Remember my friend's singing teacher saying you fall into the high notes? Sometimes, our culture of structured time and busyness makes us think we need permission to claim space for ourselves to rest, don't we? I am so guilty of saying to my children: "I'll be with you in a second. I just want to ..."

When we experience space, we often fall into our true self, without planning it. Something happens when we have space. Soulfulness is about space. When we have real space, we can become more available to ourselves.

Jon Kabat-Zinn calls it the challenge of "voluntary simplicity" – to just do one thing at a time and to really be present when you do it.

I just want to do what? Can't it wait? Is it really that important?

Robin Sharma, in his book *The 5 AM Club: Own Your Morning. Elevate Your Life*, said:

> *Growth happens in the resting phase.*

We do not grow when we go at full speed. We do not develop if we never stop. It is in the space between the rushing – in the resting – that we grow. Neuroscience tells us that the neurotransmitters re-fire during the resting phase. Our sub-conscious processes work while we are sleeping, that we have learned from Carl Jung. Our immune system reboots when we are resting. It is all about space.

Remember the liminal space in the desert that brings transition and growth? The desert is not a place where things happen quickly. It is a place where you need to slow down and wait patiently, a place with an abundance of space. This is where you can fall into your true, soulful self. But to "fall into your true self" you need space – and space is becoming scarce in this day and age. Space is the container.

Furthermore, the lack of space in our outside world can translate into a lack of space in the inner world, and *vice versa*. We can see this in the way that people live and work. This can cause anxiety, stress, and pent-up anger. This suffocates the inner voice. When this happens, the body wants to act out in other ways.

The silence of the inner voice

Brian Draper said:

In the turbulent world the answer is in the inner life.

This is so true. The interplay between our inner life and outer life is often under much pressure. Often, I am unaware of the inner voices and drivers that want to speak up against what happens in my outer life. But the pressure to conform, control and compete is so strong that it silences this voice. It brings disconnection between the true self and the social self. We get disconnected from what is important to us and what matters most. And this is a daily challenge!

How do we survive in this turbulent world? A part of the answer is hidden in a deeper life. Living a deeper life does not mean stop living the life that you are in; it simply means to live life differently. Soulfully.

Richard Rohr wrote the following in *Falling Upward*:

Maybe people are not either-or thinkers, but they bathe in the ocean of both-and ...

This is part of my challenge – my struggle to live in the both-and world. We always want a solution. When I am helping people, I am giving them solutions. I am *doing* something for them; I am solving their problems, if you like. They need me. I always want to help, and when I succeed my ego feels great. Who is it really about, then?

In the process of spiritual formation, thinkers like Richard Rohr and James Hollis referred to the difference between the content of life and the container of life. Hollis said that in the "first half of life" we spend time to create a container and structure. Then, later in life, we try to fill the container with content. Hollis talked about the first and second half of life – first half being the time when you develop sufficient ego strength and second half when you ask the question, "What matters most?" Soulfulness is about staying close to what matters most to you, even from early life. Soulfulness is about finding ways to stay close to this question: "What matters most?" But it is difficult to cultivate soulfulness without a proper container. Richard Rohr said in his book Falling Upward:

> *You need a very strong container to hold the contents and contradictions that arrive in later life.*

Soulfulness is a way to create a container – to cultivate space in your life. But how can you use it?

Soulfulness is a container with space. This I do believe! Soulfulness is a container of habits and responses in the outer life that holds the contents and awakenings of the inner life. We create space in the outer ways of life through our habits and continuous responses. These outer spaces will slowly translate into inner spaces. In the world of turbulence and speed, this space often needs to be scheduled (unfortunately), initially anyway. Rohr profoundly asked:

> *Do you choose growth (2nd half) or security (1st half)? You cannot have both!*

Life is a continuous conversation and daily choice between growth and security. Do I spend my money to do something wild and creative that will help me grow, or do I hold onto the money to be more secure? This is a daily choice: growth or security? Yet, we need both!

This is what I have realised: I cannot force people towards their "content" or meaning. I cannot "help" them to understand or grow. I can only create a container (space) for them to find the contents themselves and to grow in their own way. It was liberating for me to realise this.

People yearn back to the simplicity of breathing and being. They want to set aside time for reflection and sense-making. They want to make their own meaning. I cannot give meaning to them through counselling, coaching or training. But I can help them to create a container where they can discover meaning themselves – it is more sustainable anyway. And I needed to be okay with that. This is what the wilderness has taught me. Create the space and then trust that the space will move to where it needs to – maybe even to an appointment with the divine Doctor.

This might be the most important concept in the work on soulfulness – creating space for the soul. Over the past few years, I have deliberately tried to create space for people and groups, and I was fascinated with the outcomes. It was difficult for me to trust this. Creating space is not passive; it is not about doing nothing and hoping for the best. It is an active and deliberate act. It requires skill and awareness. And the ability to follow the energy.

It asks of us to suspend the need for instant outcomes and things to do. It challenges us to be in the space and to believe it will bring us wisdom and action when the time is right. It asks of us to fall into the true self. The space we create in the outer life is connected to the space we have inside of us, and *vice versa*.

Cultivating space

Can we be more intentional about space? How do we fill our spaces and cultivate the privilege to experience space externally and internally? My greatest learning in this soulful journey was around space – the experience of inner and outer space, and how I deliberately cultivate those spaces. I have discovered a few basic principles and themes about space.

I would humbly like to share a few learnings on how to create space, based on my work with individuals and teams.

Disengage / engage

Life is a balancing act. Sometimes, when we are on the run, it is difficult to stop and smell the roses. A colleague once told me: "Do remember, even if you win the rat race you are still a rat!"

For me the challenge to live soulfully is to live "engaged". This means to live with awareness and space, from moment to moment.

Tony Schwartz, founder and CEO of The Energy Project ("manage your energy, not your time"), and co-author of *The Way We're Working Isn't Working*, made the following profound statement:

> *Instead, we live in a gray zone, constantly juggling activities but rarely fully engaging in any of them – or fully disengaging from any of them. The consequence is that we settle for a pale version of the possible.*

A pale version of the possible – isn't that profound? Life has conned us into settling for a lesser version of ourselves, and we are not even aware of it. How many times have I sat with my children without really being there? Worrying about the future (read: the budget), the next work challenge, or the last instant news article that I read on my phone (before bedtime!). Instead, I should have been engaged in the moment, seeing their energy. The challenge for me is to really disengage from my previous engagement, to deliberately leave my previous task, to switch off the phone and put it down – simple stuff indeed. In my work with organisations I often help people to deliberately disengage.

Maybe next time you can deliberately disengage before you engage so that you do not settle for a pale version of what is possible. Disengage from the grey zone of life. Go for colourful, vibrant and engaged. Moment to moment. Believe me, it is there!

Relationships

Life is about relationships. Life and work are relational. We relate all the time. We are in a relationship with nature, with belief, with people, and with experience.

It is important to create space in this relational realm. We need space to really listen, to be there, and to be aware of our own experiences, expectations and longings. Like Jon Kabat-Zinn said, we need to be available to the energy in the room.

Nature

For me, there is nothing like nature to experience space. When I enter nature deliberately, I am aware that I am part of something bigger. My experience of God's presence is so connected to nature. Over the past few years, I have increasingly incorporated nature experiences – space – in the teamwork that I do with organisations.

James Hollis said: "As children we listened to the sound of the sea still echoing in the shell we picked up by the shore. That ancestral roar links us to the great sea which surges within us as well."

> TRY THIS:
>
> Deliberately go into nature and find a place that is a little elevated. Stand there and look at the vast space in front of you. Be open and available to what happens. Just be open to what emerges for you.

Neurological findings

Neurology and space: There is more opportunity for creativity in a boardroom with a very high ceiling. Deliberately think about your workspace. How do you personalise it? The company Neurozone was founded based on the research of Dr Etienne van der Walt about the different drivers in the brain that influence performance. He identified 11 drivers within the brain, one of which he calls sensory integration. Sensory integration refers to how your external space and surroundings influence your ability to perform. Maybe you have some family photos on your desk that makes your space personal, or a painting at work that "really speaks to you". Maybe it is a certain colour, or the height of the ceiling in the boardroom. Therefore, be intentional about your workspace. It matters, and it influences your ability to perform.

Noise and silence

Nothing creates space like silence. Is there any way in which you can create more spaces of silence in order to be open to what might happen? We live in a world full of noise. This includes visual noise like billboards, messages that appear on your phone, and music in public places.

> TRY THIS:
>
> Find a place where you can sit in silence for 5 minutes every day, and see what happens.
>
> TRY THIS:
>
> Start your board meeting with 2 minutes of silence. Then ask people what they have experienced. Your ego will tell you it is a silly exercise but do it anyway.

Discipline and rhythm

Space is about rhythm. Rhythm helps to create space and awareness. When we move too fast or too randomly, we miss the spaces.

> *"The rich invest in time, the poor invest in money."*
> – Robin Sharma

Although I will not see myself as a disciplined person, soulfulness helped me to realise the importance of discipline or rhythm. When I create space in terms of my time, it helps me to "fall into my true self".

> *"It is well to be up before daybreak, for such habits contribute to health, wealth and wisdom. –* Aristotle

In my own journey over the past year I have challenged myself to start my day differently. I have never been an early-morning person. However, I am trying to create a container of space for myself by getting up before anybody else and using this space for reflection and learning. I have found that this rhythm sets me up for the day. This is not about being a disciplined person – for 45 years I could not get up early for any reason. But the deliberate space is helping me to build capacity.

I have truly experienced the "rhythms of grace" that Brian Draper referred to in his book *Soulfulness: Deepening the mindful life*.

Gratitude and affirmation

In a recent coaching discussion, we talked about ideas to bring the positive into the present. Shawn Achor uses a gratitude diary as a way to deliberately create space for gratitude. You do this by writing down each day what you are grateful for and keeping track of that.

I once coached a woman when the topic of significance – and the person's need for significance – was raised. She came up with the idea of a "significance diary" – to have a separate journal in which to capture moments of significance every day, even in the most ordinary situations. What a great idea! A few days later I received an email from her quoting American management guru Tom Peters on business management practices: "Excellence is not an aspiration. Excellence is what you do in the next five minutes."

Leadership and space

In my work with leadership teams, I have learned that space is one of the scarcest resources for leaders. Space as well as time. Leaders often crave space for themselves – space in which to disconnect and build capacity through inner work. But then, when they have space, they feel the obligation to fill it with tasks and accomplishments, feeling guilty for doing nothing. I believe that the intentional creation of space is one of the key attributes of a good leader. Deliberately fight the "doing" function and do not feel guilty to use the space to discern. Quiet reflection and being is so important.

Peter Drucker said the following: "Follow effective action with quiet reflection. From the quiet reflection will come even more effective action."

Soulful leadership is not about training and coaching. It is about creating space and facilitating the space – the spaces in between, if you like. It is about translating what happens for leaders in that space into small, practical, and sustainable habits. Leaders need space in which to slow down and stay close to what they believe in, away from an ego-driven world.

Also, there is almost no room for error in a world driven by competition and egos. There is no space for failure. Soulful leaders create space for their employees in different ways. When employees have space in which they can be themselves and in which they can fail creatively, they will stay with your organisation for longer. And when leaders model this ability, and create space for themselves and others, the organisational culture will be changed for the better.

It's Christmas in November

Every year in early November I invite a few executive leaders for a leadership retreat called "Christmas in November".

This came about as a result of my own experience of the second half of each year which is characterised by rushing, running around, mindlessness and lack of space. A few years ago, I realised that towards the end of the year we push hard to get things done. We do not look after ourselves. And when the December holidays come, we crash. This means that the last three weeks of the working year is full of deadlines and last-minute pressure. Come December we are so exhausted and disengaged that we cannot enjoy the holiday properly – we are not present. And before we know it is January, and the cycle starts again.
I realised that we need to deliberately slow down before the year-end rush in order to stay engaged, finish our work properly, and still have capacity to engage in the holiday time. Think for a moment: How many

times have your family told you during your holiday that you are not present? It is really challenging to be in the moment when you have crashed into your space.

This was a real challenge for me to deliberately slow down, reflect on the year and re-align with what matters most. This is part of the ability to live a soulful life. So don't wait for Christmas to align and recharge – start early.

Life and space

In life, we yearn to have a space to which we can return – a space for those things that matter most to us: silence, family, friends, the self. It requires discipline to create this space.

In one of his Lent reflections, Brian Draper, referred to an article from the lifestyle website Wawaza about the Japanese minimalist concept of *Ma*. *Ma* honours the space between things. While the world is full of clutter and lack of space, *Ma* focuses on the presence of space instead of the absence of clutter. This *Ma* concept creates intentional space like a *container within which things can exist, stand out and have meaning*. It is ironic that in the West we do not have a term for this deliberate space between things. Maybe this is something we can develop in life and work – like the silent spaces between the notes in a piece of music. Maybe we need the Japanese culture to help us find a concept, word or habit for this – soulfulness wants to create such spaces.

And space is often surprising.

I recently conducted a team day with a group that I have known for a good number of years. Normally I will start with music and a breathing exercise, allowing them to "check in" with themselves and each other. On this specific day, there were a few new people in the group, and I thought they might find the exercise strange. So, I decided not to do it. During teatime, one of the regular group members came to me and said: "I was so looking forward the whole week to the silence and breathing exercise. Why didn't you do it? Is something wrong?"

This was the person I least expected it from. Again, I was encouraged to keep creating this container with breathing and music, and to be intentional about it. After teatime, I decided to do this exercise, allowing the people to reflect with music. This is confirmation that space is precious and even sacred for people.

In August 2017, when I spoke to my own coach and mentor about my ability to build capacity, he told me to block out a day in my diary for November ... this is how Christmas in November was born. I was surprised how my own longing for inner space translated into a concept and programme that now helps to create space for other leaders.

But is it realistic?

It is great to talk about creating space, Christmas in November, and sitting under a tree. But is this realistic? Thinking about my experience about Christmas in November, and creating space for reflection and nothingness, I know it is a real privilege to have space. In South Africa, most people rush around in order to survive – not because they want to but because they do not have the luxury of slowing down and pausing. The mindless race is part of life as we know it. If I tell them to take a day off for Christmas in November, will they laugh at me? Or if you start your next board meeting with a moment of silence, how will that create space for people? What other ways are there to create space? I have learned that often when you facilitate space for people, they become more aware of things that are uncomfortable. What might the answer be?

I am keen to learn from others how we can cultivate this space. It must be possible to find small and simple but realistic ways to do this.

Water drop: Inner life

The answer is in the inner life. The answer is in finding a way to cultivate your purpose, your identity as well as your impact. We need to find soulful ways to live an integrated life and to stay close to what matters most to us. Life tends to take us away from this.

I have learned that it is about taking small, practical, and realistic steps every day, to be intentional about what is significant, and to stay human in the process. Spirituality is about waking up, not about sleepwalking through life.

So, what is the realistic new normal if a random droplet of water could stop me in my tracks, if I have realised a few things along the way through my ego talk, if I have realised it is not about me, and if I know that space makes me rich? These awakenings are all good, but life happens, and you need to remain realistic, right? This is how the penny dropped for me: It is not about taking myself away from life – the drop of water fell from the sky into my context and my space while I was running. Nothing changed but everything changed. The drop of water found me in my life. Where is it finding you?

What is your drop of water?

REFLECT AND RESPOND

Here is another exercise I've learned from Brian Draper, the author of the 40-day email series. Try and find a big tree (with leaves) in your area where you can spend 15 minutes. Sit under the tree and gently start to look up to the crown of the tree. Deliberately try to focus on the spaces between the leaves instead of the leaves themselves. If you intuitively shift your focus back to the leaves, simply bring your focus back to the spaces in between. Often, when we focus on the task at hand, we miss the spaces in between. Often, too, with our family members and team members, we struggle to be available and to just be in the space with them, and to create space together.

Write down your response:

I woke up to _____

and therefore I will _____.

10.
The way back

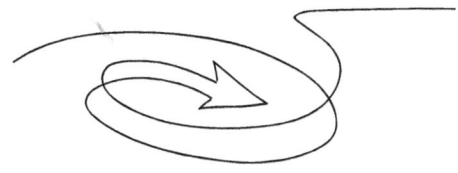

People need to human, man!

SERVAAS KRIEK

In February 2018 I spent a day with an executive leadership team, not foucsing on skills training as usual but rather going through a few contemplative practices together. We walked a labyrinth and talked about the exco members' purpose, their energy management, spent time in silence and reflection, and enjoyed good food together. This was not a strategic session or management training – it was about time and space to re-align with themselves, what they are about, and their purpose, making sure that they care for themselves and for each other. A few days later I received the following message from the Group CEO:

> *This soulful leadership time with the team was so special; it will be remembered long after all the deals and challenges.*

Maybe it is possible to keep it simple. We simply created meaning together because meaning is the new money. We created space for shifts to happen. It was in the small, simple human acts that we found our purpose and found each other.

There is a big difference between moving at speed in an engaged way versus going so fast that you become absent and disengaged.

Remember Tony Schwartz's reference to a grey zone where we are living in between engage and disengage? When we do this, we settle for a pale version of the possible because we cannot do what Jon Kabat-Zinn calls voluntary simplicity – choosing one thing and really be there for it.

Do I choose growth or security?

After participating in an "energy workshop", a small-business client of mine decided to start their meetings in a different way. The person who chairs the meeting will start with 5 minutes of time for people to properly disengage from what they were busy with – even finishing an email. At the end of the meeting, they will again get 5 minutes to really disengage. Maybe it is possible to keep it simple!

I often wonder where I am running to. Why am I going so fast, and what am I missing along the way? There is nothing wrong with speed.

We need to produce outputs and some of us get a lot of energy from the pressure, but what is the cost in terms of life quality? Again, the Japanese concept of *Ma* (remember the word from the previous chapter) wants to engage with intentional space and transition. The author of the 40-day email series wrote in one of his Lent reflections:

> *Worry less about leaving with clear answers; consider instead cultivating one wise question – opening up space in time for higher, wider, deeper truth about life in this mind-expanding, heart transforming, game changing kingdom of God.*

Cultivating one wise question – that could be a plan. This is one way to cultivate space. Instead of giving in to the culture of quick fixes, maybe cultivate one wise question every week?

The way back?

So, what is the way back to ourselves, our time, our own significance and our own wisdom? Is it possible to keep it simple? Why should we develop consciousness, go back to presence, significance, meaning and purpose? We need to find a way back to ourselves in life and work – back to our human team members. Is integrity a way back to ourselves?

In his book *21 lessons for the 21st century*, Yuval Noah Harari wrote about the challenge of being human in a technological age:

> *If we are not careful, we will end up with downgraded humans misusing upgraded computers to wreak havoc on themselves and the world.*

Our ability to be human is under pressure. The ability to still see and experience beauty without pulling out our smartphones to take a picture and share it is under pressure. Harari continued:

> *We have been losing our ability to pay attention to what we smell and taste.*

He uses the example of how easy it is to talk to your cousin in Switzerland – but not to your husband around the breakfast table, especially if he is engaged on his phone. The ability to stay awake and ethical is becoming harder and harder. It is like the sleepwalking that Anthony de Mello talks about. It will not go away. We will have to find a way to cultivate soulfulness within the busyness, to create space amidst all the distractions. Ethics is part of this. So are intentional spaces, water drops to keep us close to what really matters, and contemplative practices. The drop of water found me, but I had to feel it as a human being and then integrate that into my next intentional step.

To be an ethical human being at work, at home or in the world asks of us to live with integrity. We need to live a life that is integrated, where we are aware of the three themes:

Purpose, identity, and impact

What am I part of, and who is God for me? (why)

Who am I? (who)

Where am I and what is my responsibility? (where)

> *A life of soulfulness is a life of integrity. Part of the answer in this turbulent world is hidden in the deeper life. Deeper life does not mean to stop living the life that you are in but to live it differently. Soulfully. A life of meaning and significance from moment to moment?*

One day, Dewitt Jones, lead photographer for *National Geographic* magazine, delivered a moving motivational speech to a corporate called Extraordinary Visions. Jones used his photography to motivate people to not look at a picture once but to keep looking because *"there is always more than one right answer"*. This is part of the journey back to ourselves and our own humanity, namely to seek for more, to look again and to wait, patiently, for beauty to show itself. Jones also stated that "beauty is God's way of staying obvious".

Jones told his audience that in every ordinary moment something extraordinary wants to show itself. We simply need to keep looking. It is there!

Human is a verb

A few years ago, I conducted a soulful leadership process with a team in the app development industry. Towards the end of the session, I asked each person to summarise one awakening from the session – something that they realised or woke up to. I always do that to try and capture the essence of what transpired for people. As we went around the room one guy who did not share a lot during the session shouted:

"People need to human, man!"

What a profound and scary statement. In a world of *doing* life, we often forget about being. We are human beings and not human doings, with good reason. In life and work we often miss the simple moments of humanity, engaging with each other and with business as human beings.

How and where can you be more human? Think about this for a bit. Where are the spaces that you need to find a way back to your own humanity?

When I check my emails during meals and lose my ability to pay attention to my own sensations, I am on a slippery slope. When I have lunch while scrolling the news feed on my phone, I will not taste my food. I will not be available to my own humanity. Yes, people need to human.

Harari wrote:

> *The danger is that if we invest too much in developing AI and too little in developing human consciousness, the very sophisticated artificial intelligence of computers might only serve to empower the natural stupidity of humans.*

We need to find a way back to ourselves, cultivating wise questions and not only instant answers. Artificial intelligence can provide us with instant answers and save us time. It will help us solve problems much quicker, and that is a good thing. But how do we cultivate human consciousness that is slower and wiser? Yes, slower but wiser.

Technology can help us to solve the problems of intelligence, but we need human consciousness and the ability to feel, experience and sense as well. Wisdom, discernment and contemplation.

A way back to your ethical self

If we live a life of soulfulness we need to regularly return to our purpose (what we are part of and why), our identity (who we are) and our impact (where we are and what difference we make). It is about returning to ourselves, really. Maybe it is human to keep asking: Why do I do what I am doing, and what I am part of (purpose)? Who am I, where do I come from, and who do I want to be (identity)? What do I want to contribute to this world (impact)? This is what soulfulness is about.

My challenge and mission are to learn how to support people from all walks of life so that they can live a life of integrity and consciousness. Creating space for this is exciting. A life of soulfulness calls for constant development into a more integrated life. Remember the Latin word *integra* – the origin of the words *integrity* and *integrate*? Maybe this is what the world is yearning for: living with more integrity and living with more wholeness, realising what you are part of, who you are and why you are here for impact.

A way back to integrity?

A soulful life is a life where you, at any given moment, can answer questions about your purpose, identity and impact. This does not mean that you will never be busy with mundane stuff. Life happens. But you will be aware of the bigger picture. You will be able to recognise the small mercies and the small victories (and celebrate them intentionally), to find beauty (and God) along the way, and you will remember what you are part of and why! This is the way back to meaning, humanity and soulfulness. Every person has the ability to do (no, to be) this.

I believe the soulful moment that was given to me with a small drop of water was a gift to realign with meaningfulness. I will now look differently at the "water drops" that come my way. I will see them as signs leading me back to being human with integrity. Integrity that makes me more whole (integra) and more human.

We are always searching for meaning. In my conversations with leaders, teams, organisations and families it is evident that everyone is searching for the same thing – meaning. I have great respect for the younger workforce members (read: millennials) who are willing to work for less money in exchange for meaning and purpose in their workplace.

A few years ago, I was in a coaching discussion with a 26-year-old software developer. Annoyed, he tried to convince me that we should stop talking about work-life balance. Fascinatingly, he said the following, which still rings in my ears today:

> *Guys like you (coaches) should not talk to us about work-life balance. I code. That is what I do, I code! Sometimes during the day, sometimes during the night, sometimes it is work, sometimes it is play. So don't tell me to stop working at 5 or to start at 8, because I code.*

And then, with a very straight face, he said the following:

> *And sometimes it is really irritating to have disruptions like eating or going to the bathroom!*

It was beautiful to see his passion for coding. He did not differentiate between life and work. His purpose was integrated and timeless. Although I had a discussion with him about the importance of managing one's energy and healthy habits like enough sleep, this was a fine example of somebody who is passionate about his work and find so much purpose in it that work and play blend into one. And the fact that he loves it means there is no problem with motivation.

Soulful relationships

The same is true for relationships – people will part with a lot of money to have a meaningful connection with somebody. A friend of mine who is 45 and single recently told me that he is willing to go and work in a mine if he can just find love. He has a big corporate job that pays well, but he just wants a simple, human connection. Indeed, the coronavirus pandemic has reminded us how important real human relationships are. People tell me how they miss simple human touch and in-person relating in a world where we have come to relate on virtual platforms. People are different though - an engineer made the funny comment that he cannot wait for social distancing rules of 1.5 meters to be cancelled, so that he can go back to his normal 3 meters. 1.5 meters is just too close he said! Yes people re different but we need human connection. In our relationships we add so much fluff and find it so difficult to return to the simple stuff. That simple connection often has nothing to do with doing but with being. It asks people to return to themselves.

Soulful family

Family life can easily turn into a blur of activities and achievements, causing us to miss those meaningful moments around the table. It is not always easy to find the time to look each other in the eye, smile and connect. I remember the reference from Jon Kabat-Zinn about how we often try to fit in another task instead of creating space to experience the energies in the moment, often the human energies. We need to think together how we can create soulful family life, and we need to think broader about family than the nucleus family. There must be opportunities for people to experience family and community in different ways. That I do believe.

Soulful families live with more meaning, integrity and soul. Family can easily become an ego exercise of achievements. How many times have people told me that they struggle to be really present in their family because of financial stress, business deals and the pressure to fit in? It is really important to sometimes just be there.

What does soulful family look like for you? How do you bring soul back into the family? How do you cultivate the space for this? What would one small step look like for you and your family?

Soulful couples

How soulful are we still in our relationships? When referring to couples I want to honour the soulful connections between people without boxing them into specific marital relationships. I am privileged to journey with couples on their relational journeys; I learn so much from each one of them about staying close to what matters most in a relationship. Even with couples it is difficult to stay close to each other amidst the pressures of each day. Not long ago I had a discussion with a couple on how to stay aligned with each other during their 40s while taking care of their small children, building their careers, and managing life. Soulfulness calls for deliberate habits to stay aligned in relationships. It calls for intentional habits and rhythms.

We define healthy couples as people who perform their roles by communicating functionally, and as people who do intimacy, fulfil each other, manage life, and are happy all the time. But is a couple relationship a place where you can just be yourself? A place with space? Or is this part of the role? How much of it is a mask that you wear to show the world that you also DO relationships properly and successfully?

Are our relationships a place where we can still be vulnerable? Isn't vulnerability the glue of authenticity in relationships? Or do I need to be somebody else?

What about spontaneity, abundance, honesty, and authenticity? This is the way back to stay aware as a couple, and to respond authentically in this space. We also need drops of water in relationships, and time to simply be present within the water-drop moments of every day.

Soulful organisations?

For a number of years, part of this journey was to think about the existence of soulful organisations. What does a soulful organisation look like?

Frédéric Laloux studied the consciousness development of organisations over the last few centuries, and developed the idea of Teal organisations. These are organisations that moved away from the hierarchic model of predict, control and command to view the organisation as an organism that senses and responds uniquely and creatively. These organisations' values focus on purpose beyond profit, and expect a system where people manage themselves. They view people as whole and want to create a sense of abundance instead of scarcity and fear. Growth is always aligned with purpose, and Teal organisations will sometimes choose growth instead of security. For me, this correlates with my understanding of a soulful organisation where the organism or ecosystem is purpose driven, and very aware of responding creatively to opportunities with relationships as key. Laloux said the following in his book *Reinventing Organizations: A Guide to Creating Organizations Inspired by the Next Stage of Human Consciousness*:

> *We do not necessarily have to lose or sell our soul to make a difference within an organisation; in fact, in the right setting, we can find and express our soul through our life's work instead.*

Work can be a soulful place – a place where you understand the interplay between ego-self and soulful-self. British leadership expert Richard Barrett said that companies either operate from the fears of the ego or the love of the soul. You have to make a choice. This is how we can build companies where purpose is the driver, and where we build an ecosystem with quality relationships and authentic conversations. As Laloux said,

> *The single most important component of an organisational culture, and of wholeness, is the quality of relationships and authenticity of conversations across your company.*

Soulful organisations should be spaces of wisdom where there is room to connect with your deeper self. Soulful organisations are relational and do business for the right reasons. Laloux again:

> *We are no longer fused with our ego, and we don't let its fears reflexively control our lives. In the process, we make room to listen to the wisdom of other, deeper parts of ourselves.*

Are you working in a soulful organisation? What does it look like for you? How does purpose drive what you are doing?

Water drop: Meaning is the new money!

Part of the way back to ourselves, our ethical selves, and a life of integrity is a redefinition of what is meaningful and important to us. Soulfulness wants to nudge us back to what is meaningful in our lives in a simplistic and realistic way. It means bringing back meaning into our relationships, families, organisations, and society because meaningfulness has become the new money – meaning is a currency. It might be wise to contemplate the cost in our own lives of always being under pressure, and the small steps we can take to become more engaged along the way. What will it cost to find the way back to ourselves and each other?

I continue to contemplate how a tiny drop of water could escalate into this journey. I know it is not simple, but I do believe with small, intentional steps we can find a way back to ourselves, to each other and to God. This will enable us to live in an integrated way with experiences of purpose, identity, and impact. This is not the final answer, but part of the journey with intentional questions.

REFLECT AND RESPOND

What sort of awareness diary do you need? What if you can keep track of the most significant experiences over the next month? It does not matter how your experience of significance compare (ego) with what society tells us about significance. It is about what is significant in your experience, and how you will respond to that. Do an audit of the soulfulness of your organisation or family by answering the following questions:

PURPOSE:

Why do we exist and what are we part of?

IDENTITY:

Who are we and where do we come from?

IMPACT:

What is the legacy or impact we want to leave behind?

How do we make a difference?

Ask one wise question a month: Start by writing down the question. Do not answer it yet. Simply leave the question there and ponder it. Remember to keep asking and to be open to more than one right answer. This might change the answer into something extraordinary.

Write down your response:

I woke up to _____

and therefore I will _____.

11.
Just start!

A soulful response derives from a gentle nudge,
a nudge of soul, where you just start
— not trying to do too much,
but just enough to shift.

Are you reactive or responsive?

There is a big difference between reacting and responding. Reactions are usually instant and impulsive while responses are more thought through and true. My challenge is to move from a life of reaction to a journey of intentional response. In any journey of awakening and transformation the challenge is to really integrate whatever has happened to you. So now, at the end of this writing, it is important for you to choose a deliberate response. I'm not suggesting that as an action step or a condescending self-help recipe. It is an invitation to find a simple, unique response.

I have learned that awakening and awareness are strengthened by consistent response. In a way, the response "cements" or reinforces the awareness. That is why we need to make a habit of finding simple ways to respond to our realisations. We tend to reflect, decide, write down, and think again without finding simple and practical ways to respond. In the world of software development and systems design they have a saying: "fail fast," from the statement "fail often, fail big, fail fast." It is a philosophy that values incremental development to determine whether an idea has value. It helps us to quickly discover what works, to save costs and to increase the chances of success. Thomas Edison "failed" 9 000 times before he successfully invented the lightbulb. It makes me think of what Richard Rohr said about transformation:

> *We do not think ourselves into new ways of living, we live ourselves into new ways of thinking.*

On our journeys to become soulful we need to find ways to respond to our awakenings. Therefore, just start somewhere and keep it going. Do not overthink or over-plan it. Just start. Sheryl Sandberg, Chief Operating Officer of Facebook, famously said: "Done is better than perfect!"

At the end of each chapter in this book there was an opportunity for you to capture what you woke up to and how you chose to respond:

I woke up to _____

and therefore I will _____.

It gave you an opportunity to think about one way to respond. At the end of this journey you'll have an opportunity to add up all your responses in creative way. This is a small but practical step to reinforce your realisations on this journey.

I hope that this can become a manifesto for you towards a new normal. Maybe you can write a slogan or a poem for yourself to summarise? At the end of this book there is a mindmap that can help you.

Be mindful, not soulful!

In 2019, I joined an online course on mindfulness-based stress reduction compiled by Dave Potter. It is based on the programme founded by Jon Kabat-Zinn at the University of Massachusetts Medical School. Potter shared a five-step model of mindfulness (by Vidyamala Burch) which is really simple. I am not a great fan of steps and models because they can easily feed into our need for instant gratification. However, this encouraged me to embark on this journey of soulfulness in its most basic form:

- The **first step** is to become more familiar with what is happening in every moment, and it is called *awareness*. The awakening by the drop of water forced me to become aware of what was happening in the moment.

- The **second step** is to move towards the unpleasant. Potter calls it leaning into *resistance*. Initially, in my own soulful journey there was resistance and questions. I was called to leave the home of my status quo and I resisted.

- The **third step** is seeking the *pleasant*. A big part of my awareness journey, especially after the experience of resistance, is choosing the pleasant and choosing the new – it is a daily choice (through synchronicity, allies and community, through the desert). It is a choice to see the beauty and celebrate what is right with the world by bringing the positive into the present.

- The **fourth step** is broadening the awareness to include both the pleasant and the unpleasant part of your experience. Potter uses the metaphor of a wide-angle lens, switching from a narrow focus to a wide view. The journey of soulfulness does not want to avoid difficulty; it wants to hold onto it with a wider perspective. Charlotte Joko Beck calls this "becoming a bigger container". Soulfulness creates a container to capture the meaning.

- The **fifth step** is *learning to respond* rather than to react. We have the freedom to choose a response and to then act on the response, which is the essence of the journey of soulfulness.

Awakening, seeing, responding.

This story started with a sense of synchronicity that happened across two continents, meeting mentors, experiencing resistance, and finding community. And then I started to respond (individually and communally). This writing is part of the response – a response that moves from mere mindfulness to soulfulness. Simple but soulful. To awake, sense and then respond with one small step.

Choose wise responses

Life is really about responding, isn't it? We can raise awareness any way we like, but in a way a life of discernment is really the ability to respond sustainably. One of the most important questions around soulfulness is how to respond to your awareness. In my own life the real challenge is not to be aware or to live with awareness – it is to know how and when to respond and to translate the response into a habit that keeps going. This is wisdom. My life's work is to respond to that little drop of water that I felt on that summer's day in February.

Let us motivate each other to choose wise responses – to stop reacting in order to respond more soulfully. This is what life and work should be about. A soulful organisation knows that it is responding to a question or a need. Organisations that are successful in the long term are organisations that are in response mode, and not only in reaction mode. They start and fail fast. Instead of command, predict and control they sense and then they respond. They know how to respond to a need in the market and they know why.

Nudge, nudge …

In 2018, the CEO of a small firm asked me to facilitate a session with one of their teams and the team of a big corporate which bought a stake in their firm as the two teams now had to work together. We designed a session to explore their collective purpose and to answer the question on why they are working together and how to find their own purpose. At that stage they worked together because "management decided this", and they wanted to find their own reasons.

I was quite anxious because I knew the smaller firm. We have worked together on soulful habits based on the more experiential nature of my work with teams. However, the big corporate was focused on outputs, and might therefore not be so keen to just be together and share experiences. I designed a process to make them walk in a nature reserve with reflective questions on their own purpose and then facilitated the *why* question in smaller groups. Later that day I overheard one of the senior members of the corporate team saying to the CEO of the smaller firm,

> "Because we had this session this morning, I trust you more".

We looked at each other and smiled in disbelief. We have not even talked about trust, but the experience together, and the designing of a collective purpose, nudged them closer together, without even speaking to each other. A soulful moment indeed. This was encouraging.

During the *2016 Shift Happens* conference I realised that shifts do not necessarily happen as a result of big changes. More often they happen as a result of small, gentle *nudges*. The inner and outer changes happen when we are able to create space for the small nudges, and when we are okay with these incremental shifts. This means we need to reframe our thinking around competition, comparison and control. We need to let go a bit. It means that maybe we should sustain the small steps and create simple solutions, rather than be overwhelmed by big personal development plans and output schedules.

To pick up on soulful nudges we need to make small adjustments and sustain these from moment to moment. The ability to listen to the gentle nudges of the soul is a spiritual process. It is a daily choice to be open to what emerges out of the moment. There may be more than one right answer. But all the while, you will be moving closer to yourself and others, expecting the extraordinary in the ordinary. This calls for an ongoing process of spiritual discernment and wise responses.

Spiritual discernment is not religion *per se* although it can include faith-based beliefs. For me, my own faith journey plays a significant part in my soulful journey. However, spirituality is a wider experience and movement than religion. It is the ability to live spiritually intelligent in the world and to discover meaning through the gentle nudges of the soul, nudges towards purpose, identity and impact. Over time, as we acknowledge these nudges and respond to them, these responses turn into habits, and habits into soul growth. It can help us to find a new way of being, a new normal.

Integrity is really about responding authentically individually and as a community

Soulful organisations, just start!

It is my dream that we create organisations that do business for the right reasons. We need organisations that do what they do based on the purpose they have ingrained into their inner life. We need organisations that have the ability to stay aware and respond meaningfully. Could this become the new normal?

Frédéric Laloux in his book *Reinventing organizations: A guide to creating organizations inspired by the next stage of human consciousness* referred to the development of organisational consciousness. He described these organisations as the new type of organisation in the 21st century. This is a conscious move away from "command and control" towards "sense and respond". Soulful organisations have the ability to sense and respond based on their purpose and context.

A while ago, I talked to a business leader about his experience of his tech development firm. I asked what they were doing, and why they were doing it. He talked about artificial intelligence and the Fourth Industrial Revolution as well as the challenges around that. His next sentence was profound: "The answer is in the inner life – that is all that is left!" Then we talked about ways to cultivate an inner life at work, especially in a world ruled by invisible algorithms.

This is wisdom. This is the response, and resurrection (if you like), that is needed. Inner life and integrity.

Simon Sinek, in his book *The Infinite Game,* refers to finite and infinite thinking. Finite thinking within organisations sticks to the known and is risk averse, while infinite thinking is more about creative and inspiring work spaces. Soulful organisations are about infinite thinking that impacts the context.

Is this realistic? Certainly not. Is it possible? Yes, it is. Soulfulness is not always realistic. Remember the crazy train journey? Soulfulness contains dreams, wisdom and imagination. If you do not hope for more, even if it is unrealistic, nothing will change.

Hindsight is 20/20

In the year 2020 the coronavirus hit the world. It forced people to "stay inside" and to think about what they were doing. It made us appreciate each day and brought a lot of humanity back into the world. It also influenced our ego spaces. Indeed, the pandemic changed our lives.

In 2021 I saw a woman in my practice after she had recovered from

Covid. She battled with anxiety and fear. During our first conversation she talked about "her second chance", saying "I am alive and feel so blessed, loved and grateful". She even decided to switch from smoking to vaping. She claimed life, and she was feeling a lot lighter after she re-assessed what she was busy with. It was an existential awakening – "Covid connects all of us," she said. For the first time she started to talk about what she could do to extend her learning to others and find purpose through that.

During the pandemic, I have made a fascinating discovery about people's ego spaces. James Hollis calls it the social self. During lockdown, and working from home, some people felt free from people distractions to focus on work. Some experienced a real loss in terms of work role, status, and place in the world. Yet, others felt less anxious as they were able to work from a truer self because with lockdown came the loss of ego space. People could no longer walk into the office thinking about their physical appearance, or share personal space while presenting their slides, or feel important because they have the corner office.

Working remotely allowed people to simply be themselves and to focus on getting the job done. Some thrived in their personal spaces while others really missed the communal spaces. Of course, there are downsides to being isolated. We need to be our social selves to feel connection, and to read facial expressions and body language.

This made me wonder: Who are you when you do not go to the office? Who are you when you only have your home and online space?

Maybe this is an opportunity to become more soulful? It is certainly an opportunity for organisations to think how they can become more soulful in a hybrid workspace.

Soulful stories

How can we cultivate families and relationships that are soulful? With family I mean any form of family (community) that you are part of in life. Is it still a soulful, authentic place?

I recently spoke to a young professor of economics at a university about the way in which life can suck authenticity and spontaneity out of you. He described how, as a child, he was full of life, abundance, and humour. Now, in his mid-thirties, he loves his job but finds it difficult to rediscover that happy child from 20 years ago. Life and ego have made everything serious. Every day, we fulfil multiple roles with less and less space in which we can simply be ourselves.

I have learned from this professor how in my own life things are often too serious because I have to perform and I have to be somebody. It is ironic the difference that a word can make – shouldn't we move from being somebody to just BE? Again, I was reminded of the pressure that our roles create, even in our closest relationships.

Soulfulness can be a way of being yourself even while performing your roles. How do we move back to ourselves? Can family and organisations become the spaces to just be without the roles and functionalities?

Soulful spirituality

Shouldn't spirituality and faith be about responding? On our faith journey we often develop practices where we react out of fear in a very legalistic way. I react because I might not be saved (fear), instead of responding because I am already saved. Do think about that.

Is it possible that religion can sometimes make spirituality soulless? I am fascinated to discover with people how to make sure that religion is soulful. To make sure that spirituality is life giving and create abun- b dance, peace and contentness without being a space of fear and guilt. To respond through your faith journey to make an impact because of the grace that you already received. To not do faith as a reactive and fearfull step, because of guilt.

Let us keep this conversation alive so that spirituality is soulful and life-giving.

Soulful leadership

Soulful leaders are authentic leaders who can simply be themselves and act from their deep selves.

Disclaimer: Leadership is not about position. We are all leaders because we all need to take responsibility somewhere in life, starting with leading ourselves. When I talk about leadership, I may therefore apply it to various levels ranging from personal leadership to leadership in the world of work.

For leadership teams, I have designed a short Soulful Leadership Journey to support them to become more aware (also of their internal conversations between ego and soul) and more integrated, and to lead from deep within.

> Soulful Leadership is about becoming more self-aware …
> It wants to support leaders to become more aware of their own capacity and energy, and to create the ability to manage their energy, not just their time.

> Soulful Leadership is about being more self-managing …
> It wants to support leaders to become more aware of why they do what they do, and to discover purpose beyond profit.

> Soulful Leadership is about being more team-oriented
> … It wants to support leaders to create teams that are accountable and that know how to co-create mutually beneficial outcomes because they are guided by the same purpose.

> Soulful Leadership is about the ability to self-govern without performance management and the ability to create feedback and accountability from within.

Nudge-nudge into the future

Indeed, it is possible that a small drop of water can change the course of one's life. It can be a sliding doors moment. The question is: What is your drop of water? Will you be aware enough to treasure this moment if it happens today?

The gentle nudges of your own soul are enough. Your inner life will carry you through.

How will you respond?

How will you respond to this book? The reading may have increased your awareness. So what?

There is one thing that you can do for yourself to help you. I want you to formulate one simple response because of the book. I want you to write your soulful manifesto, your integrity manifesto. I believe this can aid success – or rather significance – in your life. Robin Sharma, in his book *The 5 AM Club: Own Your Morning. Elevate Your Life*, said:

> *Being successful without feeling soulful is the highest of defeats.*

Sharma links the experience of being successful with the experience of being soulful. Soulfulness and success should always be aligned. And it starts with us. To live and lead with integrity, through small simple intentional steps.

REFLECT AND RESPOND

Answer the following questions:

What is one thing that you became aware of while reading this chapter?

One way to respond to this is to start doing or stop doing.

How or when will you keep yourself accountable?

Set a reminder.

Be soulful!

And what is the ONE THING that you just need to start with?

Work on your integrity manifesto by going back to each chapter and collecting your "I woke up to ... and therefore I will ..." sentences.

Be creative. Now is the time to respond in your own unique way.

Write this in your own way and capture what it means to you.

Write a song, a poem, or draw a picture. You can use the mindmap at the end of this book as a map.

12.
Reflections from the author

I finished the first draft of this book towards the end of April 2020 at the start of a worldwide lockdown due to the coronavirus. In South Africa, the lockdown started with an initial 21-day period during which only shopping for essential food and medical supplies was permitted. Three weeks at home with the family. Suddenly there was TIME for things that have been postponed for months – home improvements, table tennis games with the kids, slow coffee moments, sorting out my 8-year-old child's Lego blocks. Even having lunch together as a family at 13:00 every day under the oak tree - for 3 straight weeks. This was scary but liminal times indeed. I believe this was a time to reset, to reflect on what matters most in life, and to re-align with what is important. Maybe this was like the desert experience.

The country, and the world, is taking a huge economic knock and will need to re-align with what is needed and what is important. The planet is sighing a sigh of relief – less pollution, less movement, less electricity usage, and less greenhouse gas emissions. It has been a time of rebooting. Apparently, the dolphins returned to Venice because the water was clear again. Air pollution dropped dramatically in Italy and in China, allowing them to see the blue sky, the mountains and the sun again. This must mean something, right?

The pandemic has also reminded us of the divisions in the world, particularly the gap between rich and poor. I can lean into it for a few weeks and be quite philosophical about the healing that has happened and the gift of time. Yet, less than one kilometre from my house people are living in 3x3 meter shacks (informal housing).

By now, the pandemic has caused millions of people to become infected and, sadly, millions of deaths. This is not a time to be philosophical or hyper spiritual. It is a time to grieve, save lives and be realistic. Yet, it can also be a time to return to soulful rhythms – space, time, relationships, different ways of working and living. The world will never be the same again. The Irish-American teacher Kitty O'Meara wrote beautifully about how time can also bring healing:

> *And the people stayed home. And read books, and listened, and rested, and exercised, and made art, and played games, and learned new ways of being, and were still. And listened more deeply. Some meditated, some prayed, some danced. Some met their shadows. And the people began to think differently. And the people healed. And, in the absence of people living in ignorant, dangerous, mindless, and heartless ways, the earth began to heal.*
>
> *And when the danger passed, and the people joined together again, they grieved their losses, and made new choices, and dreamed new images, and created new ways to live and heal the earth fully, as they had been healed.*

We found the source of Kitty O'Meara's quote on her website called The Daily Round. This is her poem about growth in times of despair. According to her, intense despair is something that forces us to realise and hopefully fix the more latent despairs inside us and to create new worlds from it. It kind of sounds like "falling upward", doesn't it? Rohr's reference to learning from falling and growing through falling. How vulnerability and falling help us sometimes to move upwards.

It is certainly a time to re-think our mindless ways. Although it has been a time of suffering, panic, uncertainty and fear, it can also serve as a liminal space (Chapter 3). From now on, we will refer to the time before Covid-19 (BC) and the time after Covid-19 (AC). The world can never go back to the way it was, can it? How do we integrate (integrity) what we have learned to change for the greater good?

Bill Gates shared the following in the midst of the pandemic, and it is reminding me how everything has spiritual value:

I'm a strong believer that there is a spiritual purpose behind everything that happens, whether that is what we perceive as being good or being bad.

As I meditate upon this, I want to share with you what I feel the Corona / Covid-19 virus is really doing to us:

1. *It is reminding us that we are all equal, regardless of our culture, religion, occupation, financial situation or how famous we are. This disease treats us all equally, perhaps we should to. If you don't believe me, just ask Tom Hanks.*

2. *It is reminding us that we are all connected and something that affects one person has an effect on another. It is reminding us that the false borders that we have put up have little value as this virus does not need a passport. It is reminding us, by oppressing us for a short time, of those in this world whose whole life is spent in oppression.*

3. *It is reminding us of how precious our health is and how we have moved to neglect it through eating nutrient poor manufactured food and drinking water that is contaminated with chemicals upon chemicals. If we don't look after our health, we will, of course, get sick.*

4. *It is reminding us of the shortness of life and of what is most important for us to do, which is to help each other, especially those who are old or sick. Our purpose is not to buy toilet rolls.*

5. *It is reminding us of how materialistic our society has become and how, when in times of difficulty, we remember that it's the essentials that we need (food, water, medicine) as opposed to the luxuries that we sometimes unnecessarily give value to.*

6. *It is reminding us of how important our family and home life is and how much we have neglected this. It is forcing us back into our houses so we can rebuild them into our home and to strengthen our family unit.*

7. *It is reminding us that our true work is not our job, that is what we do, not what we were created to do. Our true work is to look after each other, to protect each other and to be of benefit to one another.*

8. *It is reminding us to keep our egos in check. It is reminding us that no matter how great we think we are or how great others think we are, a virus can bring our world to a standstill.*

9. *It is reminding us that the power of free will is in our hands. We can choose to cooperate and help each other, to share, to give, to help and to support each other or we can choose to be selfish, to hoard, to look after only our self. Indeed, it is difficulties that bring out our true colours.*

10. *It is reminding us that we can be patient, or we can panic. We can either understand that this type of situation has happened many times before in history and will pass, or we can panic and see it as the end of the world and, consequently, cause ourselves more harm than good.*

11. *It is reminding us that this can either be an end or a new beginning. This can be a time of reflection and understanding, where we learn from our mistakes, or it can be the start of a cycle which will continue until we finally learn the lesson we are meant to.*

12. *It is reminding us that this Earth is sick. It is reminding us that we need to look at the rate of deforestation just as urgently as we look at the speed at which toilet rolls are disappearing off the shelves. We are sick because our home is sick.*

13. *It is reminding us that after every difficulty, there is always ease. Life is cyclical, and this is just a phase in this great cycle. We do not need to panic; this too shall pass.*

14. Whereas many see the Corona / Covid-19 virus as a great disaster, I prefer to see it as a *great corrector*.

It is sent to remind us of the important lessons that we seem to have forgotten and it is up to us if we will learn them or not, according to Gates.

The world is longing for human beings living with integrity, looking after themselves and one another, and the earth's resources. May there be water drops along your way! Go and find them, be open to them and make the most of them! Respond to them in a deliberate, simple, but soulful way.

Go well and be soulful!

Andre

You are welcome to share your stories with me

andre@besoulful.co.za

PAGE BACK TO EACH CHAPTER'S PERSONAL REFLECTION
AND CREATE YOUR OWN MANIFESTO

MY INTEGRITY MANIFESTO

I woke up to

_____

_____

_____

_____

_____

_____

_____

and therefore I will

_____

_____

_____

_____

_____

_____

_____

The water drop

_____
_____
_____
_____

Who's calling?

_____
_____
_____
_____

A mentor

_____
_____
_____

_____
_____
_____

It found us _____   *Shift happens*

_____

References and further reading

Campbell, J. (2014). *The Hero's Journey: Joseph Campbell on His Life and Work.* Novato, CA: New World Library.

Csikszentmihalyi, M. (2008). *Flow: The Psychology of Optimal Experience.* New York: Harper Perennial Modern Classics.

Draper, B. (2017). *Soulfulness: Deepening the mindful life.* London: Hodder & Stoughton.

Draper, B. (2000). Soul runner [YouTube video]. https://www.youtube.com/watch?v=Z-RUSq0tmgY

Draper, B. (2009). *Spiritual Intelligence: A new way of being.* Oxford: Lion Hudson.

Harari, Y. N. (2018). *21 Lessons for the 21st Century.* New York: Random House.

Hollis, J. (2006). *Finding Meaning in the Second Half of Life.* New York: Avery.

Hollis, J. (2008). *What matters most: Living a more considered life.* New York: Avery.

Hollis, J. (2018). *Living an examined life: Wisdom for the second half of the journey.* Louisville, CO: Sounds True.

Hollis, J., & Rosen, D. H. (2002). *The Archetypal Imagination.* College Station: Texas A&M University Press.

Khanna, R., Guler, I., & Nerkar, A. (2015). Fail Often, Fail Big, and Fail Fast? Learning from Small Failures and R&D Performance in the Pharmaceutical Industry. *Academy of Management Journal*, 59(2), 436-459.

Killian, AP. (2015). *Spiritual Intelligence and the content of faith: a post-foundational, interdisciplinary and hermeneutical dialogue between Danah Zonar and Dallas Willard.* Stellenbosch University.

Laloux, F. (2014). *Reinventing organizations: A guide to creating organizations inspired by the next stage of human consciousness.* Brussels: Nelson Parker.

Louw, D. J. (2004). *Mechanics of the human soul.* Stellenbosch: Sun Press.

Louw, D. J. (2012). A theological model for pastoral anthropology within the dynamics of interculturality: *Cura animarum* and the quest for *wholeness* in a *colo*-spirituality. *In die Skriflig/In Luce Verbi, 46*(2). http://dx.doi.org/10.4102/ids.v46i2.57

Moon, G. (2015). *Eternal Living: Reflections on Dallas Willard's Teaching on Faith and Formation*. Downers Grove, IL: IVP Books.

O'Meara, C. (2021). The daily round: Living from the spirit level [blog posts]. https://the-daily-round.com/

Rohr, R. (1999). *Everything Belongs: The Gift of Contemplative Prayer*. Chestnut Ridge, NY: The Crossroad Publishing Company.

Rohr, R. (2009). *The Naked Now: Learning to see as the mystics see*. Chestnut Ridge, NY: The Crossroad Publishing Company.

Rohr, R. (2011). *Falling upward: A spirituality for the two halves of life*. Hoboken, NJ: Jossey-Bass.

Rohr, R. (2013). *Immortal diamond: The search for our true self*. Hoboken, NJ: Jossey-Bass.

Rohr, R. (2020). *The Second Half of Life*. Chestnut Ridge, NY: The Crossroad Publishing Company [YouTube video]. https://www.youtube.com/watch?v=YngpUoh2AxU

Sharma, R. (2018). *The 5 AM Club: Own Your Morning. Elevate Your Life*. New York: HarperCollins Publishers.

Sinek, S. (2019). *The infinite game*. London: Portfolio Publishing.

St. Teresa of Avila. (2007). *The Interior Castle*. Mineola, New York: Dover Publications.

Schwartz, T., & Gomes, J. (2010). *The Way We're Working Isn't Working*. New York: Simon & Schuster Audio.

Willard, D. (2012). *Renovation of the heart: Putting on the character of Christ*. Colorado Springs, CO: NavPress.

Zohar, D. (2000). *Spiritual Intelligence: The Ultimate Intelligence*. London: Bloomsbury Publishing.

www.ingramcontent.com/pod-product-compliance
Lightning Source LLC
Chambersburg PA
CBHW070048100426
42734CB00040B/2788